Robert Brescia

Presented to:

Ferris Public Library

Destination Greatness

Creating A New Americanism

You didn't break it and it's not your fault,
but _we_ will fix it together!

ROBERT BRESCIA

∞ INFINITY
PUBLISHING

ISBN 978-1-4958-1238-5 (Paperback)
ISBN 978-1-4958-1237-8 (Hardcover)
ISBN 978-1-4958-1239-2 (eBook)
Library of Congress Control Number: 2016915940

Copyright © 2016 by Robert Brescia

All rights reserved, including the right of reproduction in any form, or by any mechanical or electronic means including photocopying or recording, or by any information storage or retrieval system, in whole or in part in any form, and in any case not without the written permission of the author and publisher.

Published October 2016

INFINITY PUBLISHING
1094 New DeHaven Street, Suite 100
West Conshohocken, PA 19428-2713
Toll-free (877) BUY BOOK
Local Phone (610) 941-9999
Fax (610) 941-9959
Info@buybooksontheweb.com
www.buybooksontheweb.com

DEDICATION

To my wife Marianne, whose counsel and advice for this book and for all things in life has kept me reaching for personal greatness. I am able to reach and exceed my goals with her steadfast support. When we left the Pentagon together, she gave up her very successful public service career at that time so that I could pursue my own. We have been talking about the New Americanism to one another for quite some time. I love you, Babe — and I look forward to continuing to experience our great New America together with you.

To our grandchildren who brighten our lives with their energy, intelligence, and love of life. Even though they live "a few states over" as we like to say, we are especially present in their lives since last year when their dad, our beloved son-in-law, lost his fight with cancer. Greg passed away on July 8, 2015 at 41 years old. Greg was truly a great American.

To my staff at The John Ben Shepperd Public Leadership Institute. We have the best team ever, all engaged in the service of Texas and the cause of leadership in the New Americanism. Clay Finley is our Associate Director, Katie Lopez handles all our events, Chloe Jackson keeps us all administratively correct, and our fabulous University of Texas of the Permian Basin (UTPB) student, Kyle Stephenson shoots and produces video in our studios.

To former Texas Attorney General John Ben Shepperd (1915-1990) who started a movement about Americanism in the 1950s. Readers will notice quite a few "John Ben-isms", quips, and quotes from this largely unsung hero as we revive the principles and values that he held so dear. It is in large measure the inspiration drawn from his many fiery and moving speeches that moved me to write about the New Americanism.

To all the JBS Institute's Distinguished Lecture Series speakers over the years that have consented to personal interviews about leadership and Americanism. They are among the most selfless and wonderful celebrities – all exemplars of the New Americanism.

To all of our many supporters and friends in Texas and elsewhere who share in our vision of an extraordinary rebirth of Americanism in our times.

BRESCIA

Contents

Dedication	iii
Contents	v
Foreword	vii
Preface	ix
I Believe in Americanism	1
Uncivil Nation: Battle Ground or Common Ground?	33
The Rise of the Political Parties	49
Long Live the Republic – Our Constitutional Bedrock	65
Sister Freedom and Brother Liberty	81
States – The Basic Building Blocks of the New Americanism	95
Defending Ourselves – New Ways to Protect Americans	107
Ethics – Doing the Right Thing When No One's Looking	129
Spirituality – The Soul of the New Americanism	139
Have Statesmanship – Will Serve	147
The Art of Disagreement – Bringing Back Debating Skills	157
Taking Care of Our Elderly – It's an American Thing.	165
The Truth about Youth.	177
Choosing the Next President – Why Leadership Matters.	195

TAKING THE NEW AMERICANISM HOME	211
REFERENCES	227

Foreword

At a time when Americans seem more divided than ever, when voices of hate drown out voices of reason, when most of us have no idea what the future holds, or should hold, Bob Brescia refreshingly outlines what needs to be done for America to reach her potential in his brilliant book **DESTINATION GREATNESS**.

In our fast paced increasingly smaller world, covered by a 24/7 news cycle with stories from around the globe, what does Americanism mean? Who are we as a nation? What is our role in the world? Are we a country that yearns for the values of yesterday, or one looking to recreate those values and ideals with a different world order in place? Is nostalgia the answer? Or is it time for a new Americanism? What would that entail?

Never have more Americans been involved in the political diatribes and acrimony that we witness today. Issues considered resolved long ago are rearing their heads to an angry and hostile citizenry. Supreme Court vacancies are not viewed through the lens of intellect and competence, but rather the lens of politics and ideology. The primacy of the Constitution is almost an afterthought.

ISIS continues on its march westward, as the argument is not as much how to defeat them, but what to call them.

Police are assassinated on our streets at the very moment they protect the rights of those who spew hatred against them.

Although America was colorblind when she elected an African American president, race relations seem never to have been more divided.

Enter Bob Brescia with a refreshing commentary on what we need to do to go forward; Humor is not lost as he likens the arguments of many to passengers in a broken down jalopy arguing about which road to take. His analysis doesn't judge but instead identifies what it means to be an American and how best to educate all of us to join in the mission to accomplish the destiny of greatness that America was meant to be.

Judge Jeanine Pirro
Fox News Channel television host –
Justice with Judge Jeanine

Preface

After publishing The Americanism of John Ben Shepperd last year, I came to realize just how much that the term has changed since former Texas Attorney General John Ben Shepperd's time—the 1950s. While John Ben was concerned with poll taxes, post-war economic recovery, the Communist *Red Menace* threat, we are concerned with immigration, inclusion, civility, and a host of new social issues. I felt compelled to research and write a book that describes what Americanism is today and how we can improve as Americans. I believed that the term greatness is bandied about without careful thought about what it really means. We can be as great as we want to be - together. Therefore, I wrote DESTINATION GREATNESS to clarify and teach what Americanism is currently and what it should be. It's a privilege to sometimes be referred to as "the Americanism guy". I promise to do my best to uphold American values.

I love Americanism because it is the glue that holds us together as individual citizens and as a team of teams. Without it, there is chaos, uncertainty, as well as the loss of familiar, reliable structure.

With it, there's the tangible hope of long-term survival as a constitutional republic. Like it or not, we live in a world where no global entity has yet to replace the nation-state system. The world is a place where almost 200 countries reside in friendship and competition with each other. They form alliances, groups, treaties, and organizations but they are still their own country first. It's very important, therefore, that the USA regain a strong footing of Americanism, serve as a world leader and exemplar. This is the job of all of us as Americans. This book reminds us of how great we were, how great we are now, and how great we can and will become.

The Americanism that flourished after World War II and also during the 1980s is not the same Americanism that we experience today. The reason for that is simple: our society has dramatically changed since those days. Solutions that worked then will not work in the second decade of the 21st century. Our world is a lot flatter and much smaller. If "the whole world is watching", as the political demonstrators chanted in Chicago during the 1968 Democratic National Convention, then you can magnify that same effect by a hundred or even a thousand in our times.

If we espouse this New Americanism with candor, openness, and a true willingness to work together for the common good, then we will succeed in our goals. The nation will survive and prosper for many years to come. The naysayers will fade away and tomorrow's leaders will emerge before our eyes. I am excited to be a part of it all and I know you will be too.

Gender disclaimer: Throughout this book, unless otherwise stated, whenever the masculine gender is used, both men and women are included.

This book is a call to action for us all. Instead of being a statement of the obvious, it is a statement about *what needs to be obvious again*. It is not a political statement or candidate endorsement — but you can apply politics to it in ways that you think appropriate. It is a thought-provoker. Most of all, it is a wake-up call to a new "morning in America" - a New Americanism.

Chapter 1

I Believe in Americanism

Mama may have... and Papa may have... but God Bless the child... that's got his own, that's got his own.
— Blood, Sweat, and Tears, 1968

"I believe in America."

In the opening scene of the 1972 blockbuster film, *The Godfather*, Italian immigrant Bonasera presents himself to Don Vito Corleone to ask for justice for his daughter who was attacked and seriously injured by two boys. The script reads:

> Bonasera: "I believe in America. America has made my fortune."

Like Mr. Bonasera, we must all learn and re-learn to believe in America. Working together, we can make America great again if we rediscover and re-capture the values and behaviors that made us great.

Americanism

Americanism is a collection of principles, values, behaviors, culture, traditions and form of government that, operating together, make us who we are as a people. They are distinctive characteristics that set us apart from other nations. They are the cornerstones that support our notions of Americanism patriotism, nationalism and exceptionalism. They have been there since the beginning of our fledgling nation and have grown throughout our history. They emerge spontaneously during periods of national strife and conflict. They recede when Americans become complacent and detached from the spirit and intent of our founders.

The American Legion mentions *Americanism* in its preamble to its Constitution:

> TO FOSTER AND PERPETUATE A 100 PERCENT AMERICANISM. Americanism is the gist of the American ideals of freedom, justice, individual rights and unfenced-in opportunities. It embraces all the freedoms we cherish and all the rights that are guaranteed to us. It is the very opposite of hatred, bigotry and intolerance. Americanism is the creed that has blazed the world-wide trail for justice, fair play and decency, belief in God, private enterprise, universal education, and progress in all

human endeavors. It puts a premium on the virtues of loyalty, patriotism, hard work and thrift.

I love quoting the American Legion's preamble because it's hard to find something like it – so clear and unambiguous about what we are as a nation and who we are as a people. We are extraordinary and exceptional because we were structured by *convention* and *principle* rather than elitism and social rank.

Even those in our history who have been steadfastly critical of our greatness, and desirous of fundamentally changing our very nature have admitted to our exceptionalism. For example, former Black Panther leader Huey Newton was a believer in dialectical Materialism, class struggle, and revolution – a modification of the classic Marxist style of Historical Materialism. Huey said this in a speech delivered to Boston College on November 18, 1970:

> I mentioned earlier the necessity for the redistribution of wealth. We think that it is very important to know that as things are in the world today socialism in the United States will never exist. Why? It will not exist because it cannot exist...socialism would require a socialist state and if a state does not exist how could socialism exist? In order for a revolution to occur in the United States,

you would have to have a redistribution of wealth away from the ruling circle.

Newton's point is that if a revolution occurred in the United States, it would have to be one that—skipped over—socialism and went directly to communism or his term, "revolutionary inter-communalism". The reason for this is that Americans have an exceptionally strong attachment to their nation. Newton's speech indicates that he himself believed that a short cut to socialism or communism would never be possible in the greatest nation in the world. Newton, as is the case with many social philosophers who buy in to the hype of a New World Order, was simply out of step with the realities and potential of the New Americanism.

Back in the day, television personality David Frost had the foresight to interview the candidates competing with one another during the 1968 primaries. It's interesting to review just a few candidates' responses to David's questions on Americanism (Frost, 1968):

> **David Frost**: What is the essence of being American really? Are there any essentially American Characteristics?
>
> **Richard Nixon**: Of the American people, yes. Americans really believe their mission in the world, if they have a mission, is not

to expand Americanism, so-called, but really to try to work for a world in which everybody can choose. The people of the United States need a dream, they need a vision, and they need a purpose larger than themselves. Leaders must take Americans to the mountain top and show them what that goal is and then see to it that we do meet that goal.

Eugene McCarthy: I think of America in the sense of its limited purpose, but of almost unlimited potential.

Ronald Reagan: I think there is a generosity inherent in the American people. I think there's also kind of a pioneer of the American. Tell us where we're supposed to be and we'll get there. This, I think, is an American characteristic. There's a third one, and this is probably the least understood in foreign countries when Americans are tourists. I think Americans are kind of like puppy dogs. They love everybody and they can't understand why everybody doesn't love them, so when they go visiting some other country, they want to walk up, knock on the door, and stick out their hand and say, "Hello, I'm Joe Smith from Arkansas".

If we maintain that America can be great again, does that imply that it is not great now? No. It is, however, a call to action to be as great as we possibly can be. We can and must rise above crippling political ideologies to reach the high ground of Americanism. In many cases, ideology and polarization are preventing us from being as great as we could be. As Americans, we have run to the extreme sides of the political continuum and we have done it within our two-party structure. It's like a football halfback who, each time he gets the ball, does an end run by choosing either right or left. I believe that sometimes we can get that first down, and eventually win the game, by going up the middle or passing the ball downfield.

No one political party or personality owns or controls our national principles and values. They are shared by all of us. All action must be predicated on values or conscious adherence to our collective good – any other reason or rationale is unethical. We are great because of this fact: Americans feel attached to nation as much as and more than many other citizens of other countries in the world today. That strong *bond to nation* makes us exceptional, along with our constitutional republic. All great Americans stand when the national anthem is played. They know that while there are flaws and problems in the way that our behaviors support our values, we owe a lot of respect to our nation and to those who safeguard it.

Our best days are the present moment and the days ahead. As the New York Yankee slugger Babe Ruth was fond of saying, "You don't win today's ball games with yesterday's home runs." As Americans, we are justifiably proud of our past and it's crucial that we teach that history to our youth but we rely on the greatness of today and tomorrow to serve as the bridge to exceptionalism in our future. We want our children and grandchildren to inherit *opportunity*. We want to pass along traditions, principles, values, and the history that made us who we are today. We want to restore America – a New Americanism that includes every legal immigrant, every citizen, and every visitor in its splendor. We must not be afraid of the mantle of greatness. It was in some ways thrust upon us, but it must be achieved and re-achieved constantly. We, all of the living American generations, are definitely up to the task.

Look Ahead

Here are some of the themes and conversations that you will interact with throughout this book:

> **The Case for a New Americanism.** There is an overwhelming desire of many Americans to reach a higher ground that could reunite us all. There is a feeling running through our social landscape of alienation, detachment, and fear exacerbated by global unrest (terrorism) and other factors. This "pulling away" phenomenon, especially by Generation X and millennials, is due to

the complexity and perceived magnitude of the task at hand – to restore a more united and great America. They have a tendency to think that the task is too massive, the resources aren't there and that they can't make a difference as just individuals. The New Americanism lays out a compelling description of a nation that "can" – a nation that ties together generations into a "team of teams" to get us to the higher ground of Americanism.

Principles, Values, and Behaviors. The hallmarks and cornerstones of the New Americanism are the time-honored values and principles that made us great in the last century. What has suffered are American *behaviors*. We betray our values too much and that has taken a toll. Behaviors must be based on values. Behaviors are the visible testament to our values. These values include, but certainly are not limited to: unity, truth, passion, perseverance, benevolence, leadership, optimism, courage, spirituality, community, inclusion, love, and civility. There are many opportunities that we all have in the New Americanism to place our values and principles into action through our own behaviors. You may have seen or heard about some or all of these values in other venues, books, and sources about the USA — that's not surprising because they are widespread in the literature. They will be written about in the future, too—hopefully!

Mutual Respect among Americans. Civility is disappearing from both the general society and the political landscape but it can be regained and strengthened. Our behaviors must become much more civil because it is the ladder on whose rungs we climb to the higher ground we call the New Americanism. Civility calls for truth-telling because respect for the truth is essential in fashioning solutions to important problems. It also builds trust among and between people. Bottom line: we need to start more *conversations*, not *altercations*.

Political Parties – The Machines of American Belief Systems. The significant growth of party politics and the political machines that make up those parties is a double-edged sword in the New Americanism. While we generally have a two-party system in the United States, we have all "run to the sidelines" of those parties and therefore the parties can't effectively include those who do not operate at the polarized extremes. The result is: those individuals separate from the party banner and either don't vote or vote for some write-in candidate who really doesn't have a chance and quite possibly takes votes away from candidates who do have good chances of winning. The primary process to select presidential candidates needs an overhaul.

Constitution. The U.S. Constitution needs a renaissance of rediscovery, more followership, and respect. Today's youth rarely enjoy the solid foundation of this exceptional document that created our nation and republic because they are not learning much about the Constitution in their schools. Therefore, discussion is developed on ways to bring back a new-found knowledge of the document that guarantees both freedom and liberty.

The National Defense. We can't hope to foster and cultivate a New Americanism without being safe in our persons both at home and abroad. I will describe what I believe to be a way to confront and overcome terrorism directed at Americans as well as the approach to a joint, combined, and allied structure to carry out this new strategy. I am also calling for the appointment of several —5-star Generals or Admirals—who would have highly privileged and near-immediate access to the President. Find out more about why this would be very beneficial in the national defense chapter of this book.

Ethics. It's simple, really. Live by a moral code that is based on principles and values, tell the truth, and don't betray the values. While easy to say, the reality is that we need many more Americans to model ethical behavior in all walks of American life. I show how this is possible in the New Americanism.

Spirituality. Yes, I am going there. Spirituality is the very essence of our humanity and what has made us the envy of the whole world. We cannot forsake it in the New Americanism. One of the greatest features of Americanism is our ability to worship in the way that we choose without persecution. Many have tried to trample over those rights. We need to reaffirm them in the New Americanism. I will show why and how.

Statesmanship. We have plenty of politicians but not enough statesmen. In this book, I will describe what a statesman is and why it's important for all politicians to aspire to be just that.

The Lost Art of Debate. However debates are structured and carried out, Americans are losing those skills. We seem to disagree with each other in emotional ways that are not based on reason and rationale. We are not teaching our youth how to disagree while still preserving the respect for each other as Americans. I show how we can fix that in the New Americanism.

Taking Care of Our Elderly. It's an American thing. We can't deteriorate into the kind of society that nearly *discards* its elderly through abandonment as opposed to empowerment. There is no place for poor treatment of the elderly in the New Americanism. We have a long way to go to turn these trends around, but I illuminate the path to take in the New Americanism.

Cultivating our Youth. Much has been said about youth, from Generation X to the Millennials. They've been slammed for attitudes and behaviors now and then. These younger generations have one of the most important tasks in the New Americanism—practice the American leadership behaviors that will usher in sustained periods of greatness for us all. They are up to the task. In this book, I talk about the ways that youth can assume the mantle of leadership, partner with the baby boomers and the elderly, and solve the tremendous challenges that face them almost every day.

You will find all these and more within this book. The New Americanism needs you – now and in the future.

Starbucks CEO Howard Schultz also believes in a restored America:

"Viewing the American Dream as a *reservoir* that is replenished with the values, work ethic and integrity of the American people, Schultz said, "Sadly, our reservoir is running dry, depleted by cynicism, despair, division, exclusion, fear and indifference."

He suggested citizens fill the reservoir of the American Dream back up, "not with cynicism, but with optimism. Not with despair, but with possibility. Not with division, but with unity. Not with exclusion, but with inclusion. Not with fear, but with compassion. Not with indifference, but with love." Clearly Mr. Schultz desires many of the same values that we also espouse for the New Americanism. He also focuses on the everyday behaviors we display that should always support our values.

"It's not about the choice we make every four years," Schultz said. "This is about the choices we are making every day." (Schultz, 2016)

The Old Americanism

The Old Americanism focused on the enjoyment of freedom by a relatively homogenous majority comprised of people with somewhat similar backgrounds and origins. There was a mainstream in society or as the political parties like to say, an establishment. You were either in or out of the mainstream of society. The love of Americanism was most shared and demonstrated by people who had comprised this majority. Many were of European descent, given the wave of immigration that took place shortly after the onset of the 20th century.

My grandfather, Antonio Brescia, left Italy to become an American in the early 1920s. He was extremely proud to be an American to his dying day at age 109. For his 100th birthday, his U.S. Congressman presented him with a U.S. flag flown over the nation's capital. He cried tears of joy and pride during the ceremonies on that day. Even though he was the president of his local Italian-American Society in Hartford, Connecticut, he espoused Americanism fully while still managing to respect the culture of the Italian society that he left behind. He created a small business, adding to the wealth of his community. He helped other immigrants to assimilate into the fabric of America. He was involved in local politics, examining all of the issues and making sure that his representative knew how he felt about them.

But the Old Americanism, like any social system, had its flaws and shortcomings. It was sometimes intolerant of those who with other-than-mainstream backgrounds. It also had a tendency to believe things without too much analysis, accepting them as truth at face value. When I was young, my mom and dad would sometimes answer questions about why things were this way or that way with, "Because that's the way it is". I would ask how we could change things and the most prevalent response was, "It's always been that way and probably always will – at least in our lifetimes." Those types of answers made me think that somewhere in America is a large secret vault where all the answers to these tough questions are contained. We only needed to find the vault and open it, thereby gaining the necessary knowledge to right the wrongs and change things for the better.

We were asked, as the youthful generations of the 20th century, to accept a lot as truth, not to do too much questioning, and then we could solve stuff later on when we would become "full-fledged adults". While this worked reasonably well in that historical context, it will never work in our times because our social landscape has changed so drastically. The entire world has gotten flatter and smaller through telecommunications and the internet. Today's youth do not accept values and principles at face value. They Google them. They pose powerful, generative questions that help them to put things into the boxes and containers of their own social experience.

In the 20th century Americanism, folks sometimes stated, "My country, right or wrong." While that is true, we have simply amplified that by accentuating the positive and increasing our mastery of principles and values. In the New Americanism we can now say, "My country, right because _____." We have in essence *rationalized* the "right or wrong" by becoming much more knowledgeable about *why we feel we are right*. If we are wrong, we fully admit it and start working to make it right – the right way. The previous ways often proclaimed, "Love it or leave it." The new ways of Americanism proclaim, "Love it and I can explain why you would want to." Again, a more positive and educated position. Come and share with us the wonderful benefits of being an American – and share also in the hard work, toil, duties and responsibilities that we all must shoulder. As the debate team members stated in the 2007 movie, *The Great Debaters*, "We do what have to do so that we can do what we want to do."

Texas Attorney General John Ben Shepperd had a great appreciation for Americanism and often talked about it in his role as president of the national Jaycees. Here is an excerpt from the October 21, 1947 edition of the Binghamton Press in which John Ben mentions the American way of life:

Let's wake up, America. Take our heads out of the sand and see things as they are, was the battle cry sounded by John Ben Shepperd, Texas, president of the United States Junior Chamber of Commerce, in his talk on the "fifth freedom" of free enterprise last night before 500 Junior Chamber members and their guests of Endicott, Johnson City and Binghamton. The meeting was held in the Spanish ballroom of the Arlington Hotel, Binghamton.

In his talk, Mr. Shepperd issued a warning against the evils and spread of Communism and detailed at some length the aims and desires of Junior Chamber members to be of service to their country and to their community. Eighty-five per cent of Junior Chamber membership in the nation saw World War Two service, he said.

Commenting on his recent tour of Europe, he said, "I found the young men of Europe dejected; they have lost hope and the incentive to produce. The American way of life is worth fighting for. We should make an everyday job of selling democracy. Sending food to save the hungry people of Europe should get Congress back on the democracy and I believe that we should get Congress back on the job. We have terrific responsibilities. It's a tough job facing us and it's going to take a lot of American grit and determination to see it through." He stressed that "the answer to those who threaten our freedom is a positive, dynamic program." The fifth freedom flight, he added, is an "attempt to mobilize the young men of America for action in those fields which will strengthen our democracy as part of this program."

"We have the responsibility of world citizenship," Mr. Shepperd concluded. We have the right to go as far as we can, developing according to our capacities as individual American men and women." The Texan told his listeners that the junior chamber's aim is to "teach a finer and keener appreciation of the American way of life.

The New Americanism

This book extolls the virtues of a "New Americanism" – a renaissance of true Americanism that appropriates the values of our past and re-installs them in our present. After all, social historians Will and Ariel Durant, authors of *The History of the World*, have stated, "The past is the present – all unfurled for analysis. The present is the past – all ready for action!"

Although there is an undeniable linkage to our great past as a nation, we simply cannot revert to the past in an effort to re-achieve current or future greatness. What will make us great again in the second decade of the 21st century is somewhat different from what made us great at various times in the 20th century. Our current context is significantly different. It is far more complex and technology has made a non-negligible impact on what we do and how we do it in today's world.

There do exist, however, some *cornerstones* of Americanism that can be lifted from the social structures of the past and emplaced in the structures we are now building and will continue to build in the future. The job of a cornerstone is to provide ample support for the entire building. Without it, the building will collapse. These intrinsic and timeless values are and will be the cornerstones of the New Americanism. These cornerstones correspond to the chapters within this book. They are not exclusive. They are simply the ones that leap to the fore in a clear and compelling way.

Seen another way, the cornerstones of the New Americanism are the basic underlying principles and values that we hold essential to our American character and which we will never deny or betray. They are who we are as a people, individually and collectively. They can be enumerated and described. Even though many Americans know them in an innate way and might not be able to describe them in somewhat academic terms, they certainly accept them, feel them, and have them inside their souls. This is the important part – as Americans we are all "subject matter experts" of our principles and values. Being a great American is to first acknowledge these principles and values and then put them into practice consistently. That's what makes one *a great American.*

Some Americans have stated that they will leave the country if a certain candidate gets elected as president. I believe that a person cannot be a great American by leaving because of disagreement with someone over policy issues. If you are thinking of leaving America, consider carefully what you are giving up. The Old Americanism left principles and values to be discovered and identified, and interpreted in various ways and manners. The New Americanism goes a lot farther in enumerating those values in clear and concise ways because they are too important not to do so. The Old Americanism places a high value on *rugged individualism.* The New Americanism says, "We greatly admire rugged individualism but we also believe in working together to make things happen." At this point, you may be thinking, "Where is he going with this?" Well just hang on to your hat as I lead you through the hallmarks and cornerstones of what a New Americanism can look like. After you're done reading and discovering these cornerstones, then join me and others in an exciting rebirth of American greatness.

American Exceptionalism

I have heard people offer the opinion that it's wrong and somewhat provocative to claim American Exceptionalism. They say that we are the same as everyone else in the world, and to think that we are somehow exceptional is prideful, naïve, or downright boastful. These opinions are wrong because they are based on an erroneous idea of *superiority* over everyone else in the world. I mostly use the term in reference to our *type of government* – a constitutional republic. We could also be exceptional in other ways too, like for our benevolence, frontier spirit, or courageous citizenry, as well as a host of other factors typically espoused as American. The fact is, however, that American Exceptionalism generally refers to the extraordinarily successful and durable form of government that has sustained us throughout our 240-year history.

America is exceptional because of our *republican ideals*. Our freedoms and liberties are guaranteed by our Constitution. We are a constitutional republic and whoever is in the minority need not worry that those in the majority will limit or eliminate our freedoms during the time that they are in the majority. That's what makes us exceptional. Our Constitution is the grand arbiter of what's permissible and what is not, through the action of the U.S. Supreme Court. Assuming that we respect our rule of law and have the means to enforce legislation and Supreme Court decisions, then no sub-group of citizens should have to worry upon a leadership change at the highest level of our country. Another important element of exceptionalism is that we weren't founded by royalty or some other ruling class. We were founded by common people, many of whom were simple farmers or tradesmen of some type.

Constitutional republics are a rarity on the world scene. Out of 196 total countries in the world today, only 11 are constitutional republics:

#	Country	Capital
1	Ghana	Accra
2	Honduras	Tegucigalpa
3	India	New Delhi
4	Mexico	Mexico City
5	Paraguay	Asunción
6	Philippines	Manila
7	Republic of Ireland	Dublin
8	Sierra Leone	Freetown
9	Somaliland	Hargeisa
10	United States of America	Washington, D.C.
11	Yemen	Sana'a

Considering the list of world countries which are constitutional republics, many were founded in the last century:

COUNTRY	DATE FOUNDED
United States	July 4, 1776
Paraguay	May 14, 1811
Honduras	September 15, 1821
Mexico	September 27, 1821
Philippines	January 23, 1899
India	August 15, 1947
Ireland	April 18, 1949
Ghana	March 6, 1957
Sierra Leone	April 27, 1961
Yemen	May 22, 1990
Somaliland	May 18, 1991

We are, therefore, the oldest constitutional republic in the world today – an achievement of exceptional proportions. We have stood the test of time and survived in our current governmental form. This gives us the right to claim American Exceptionalism.

American Exceptionalism is therefore a *quality*, as opposed to an ideology. As a national quality, we should never apologize for being exceptional – it is what it is. Our federalist system ensures checks and balances between the states and the federal government, and between the branches of government so that one branch does not become more powerful than another. It is a strong federation – not a loose conglomeration of states. This fantastic system makes for an exceptional American arrangement and an excellent platform for global leadership.

The United States continues to exercise a role in world leadership, as Reagan - Bush speechwriter Peggy Noonan says, because it is exceptional. She states, "America is not *exceptional* because it has long attempted to be a force for good in the world, it attempts to be a force for good because it is *exceptional.*"

American Nationalism

American nationalism is the degree to which we all identify as a nation, together as citizens. We are Americans first, then all of the other characteristics we sometimes feel compelled to bring up, such as ethnicity, national origin, etc.

It wasn't always that way. Americans didn't always feel like Americans first. These ideas came soon after the Civil War was concluded. Before that time, an American identified most often with his state, the Union, or the Confederacy.

Nationalism seems to peak coincidently with extraordinary national events, such as our participation in World Wars, or the September 11, 2001 attack on our homeland.

Nationalism is almost always based on people having a common language and culture. The Old Americanism held a belief that once a person immigrated here, there was an unwritten requirement to jump into the "melting pot", so that one would take on a single language and culture. Understanding the real nature of diversity is essential in the New Americanism. We want assimilation, not separation. We want all of our valued immigrants to begin their American lives by learning who we were, who we are, and who we want to be – together with them.

American Patriotism

American patriotism differs only slightly from American nationalism in that it focuses on the degree of attachment that Americans have to their Constitution. A "patriot" strongly believes, for example, in the primacy of the United States Constitution in solving the various social issues of our current times.

"The American's Creed" is the title of a resolution passed by the U.S. House of Representatives April 3, 1918. It is a statement written in 1917 by William Tyler Page as an entry into a patriotic contest.

I believe in the United States of America, as a government of the people, by the people, for the people; whose just powers are derived from the consent of the governed; a democracy in a republic; a sovereign Nation of many sovereign States; a perfect union, one and inseparable; established upon these principles of freedom, equality, justice, and humanity for which American patriots sacrificed their lives and fortunes. I therefore believe it is my duty to my country to love it, to support its Constitution, to obey its laws, to respect its flag, and to defend it against all enemies.

Principles and Values

Before going further, I'd like next to draw a minor distinction between principles and values. For our purposes, a *principle* is a universal, widely-held belief – a superset of values. A *value* is a principle that one has adopted and prioritized among principles. Therefore, a set of national values are those principles that we have selected and prioritized as the most important ones. These are the values that we must never betray.

A *behavior* is when we act on either a principle or a value. We are plenty interested in behaviors because of our universal principle of ethics – doing the right thing. Any behavior that is not rooted in or based on principles or values is an unethical behavior. For example, if a President is content with writing and issuing executive orders over a long period of time – and this behavior is a substitute for the principle of checks and balances and the legislative process, then such behavior could be considered unethical because it betrays one of our time-honored principles.

Ideology

Political ideology is a worldview or vision. Individuals can subscribe to particular worldviews and sometimes bind together in groups to do so. While it's normal to have a particular view of how the world should work, what the role of government should be, or other areas of human behavior, the danger is one of "I'm totally right about my worldview, and you are totally wrong."

When ideology meets authoritative power, we usually get into big trouble. For example, it was discovered in 2013 that a high-level IRS director, Lois Lerner, had allegedly created target lists of organizations for "special management" – and not in a good way. These were all conservative and/or religious organizations that did not align with her own worldview, such as Tea Party non-profits. Although there was a tenuous linkage between what Ms. Lerner was accused of doing and official IRS policy, it was clear that companies were being targeted for their particular beliefs and views. She resigned from the IRS and a subsequent investigation did not reveal enough substantive material or evidence for criminal prosecution by the Justice Department.

Consider the case of MSNBC television host, Melissa Harris-Perry when she recently walked off of her show set – physically walked away during a live shoot. This was in protest of the network pre-empting two weekends of her show in favor of covering the political primaries. Instead of going to her boss and complaining about it as a rational person would have done, she impulsively walked away, issuing the following:

"I will not be used as a tool for their purposes," she wrote. "I am not a token, mammy, or little brown bobble head. I am not owned by Lack, Griffin or MSNBC. I love our show. I want it back." (Concha, 2016).

This is some fairly incredulous language coming from a well-known political commentator talk show host on a network that might be considered as fairly diverse. Many Americans teach their children not to employ discriminatory language terms such as the ones she employed as an adult in the public eye. Maybe Ms. Harris Perry's parents did not teach her those same skills. It is inconceivable that a person who is also a Presidential Chair Professor of Politics and International Affairs at Wake Forest University, as well as a columnist for *The Nation* would act in such a childish, uncivil manner.

However, that's what we are faced with today – people who don't take the time to reflect before acting and television hosts who act in their own best interest, not in the interests of their viewers.

Ideology is conceivably the greatest crippler of our times and usually runs contrary to the cornerstones of the New Americanism. Ideology has polarized our citizens, boxing them needlessly into artificial containers that we refer to as the Democratic and Republican political parties. Don't believe me? How concerned are many Republicans with notions about saving our republic? After all, they are supposed to be Republicans. How focused are they on upholding and protecting the supreme law of the land as expressed by our superlative Constitution? How interested are many Democrats in creating a truly tolerant and egalitarian society when they are often seen creating the very same divisions and distinction among people that cause unrest and unhappiness? How can a Democrat claim that he or she is interested in creating economic and financial opportunity for small businesses to grow when that same Democrat is a fierce proponent of large government and crippling regulations?

The New Americanism is no friend of ideology. A New American is someone who places principle first, not party platform or party leadership. Ideology is better left to conversations at home or individual reflection. It should give up its driver's seat and take another seat, as a passenger, elsewhere in the vehicle. As the judge said in the final scenes of the 1947 film *The Son of Rusty* (Landers, 1947), "If the structure of American tolerance falls, we fall with it."

I've already described what it is to be a great American. A great American is not an ideologue. He reaches across the ideological divide to others in the way that President Ronald Reagan and Speaker of the House Tip O'Neill reached across to each other to make things happen. Do not confuse being a great American, however, with being a patriot. One cannot be a patriot unless he holds a belief in the primacy of our U.S. Constitution, its values, and then shows that in his daily behaviors – that's what being a patriot is.

In conclusion, I think former Texas Attorney General John Ben Shepperd captured the essence of Americanism in his own way. The following lines are how he ended many of his extraordinary speeches:

> *The greatest fault of the American people is our materialism and lack of real concern for good government. Half of us are trying to buy all the good things of life with money and the other half are trying to vote them into existence.*
>
> *But who can open a safety deposit box and file away a title to an American sunset?*

Who can lay gold on the counter and buy the look of trust and innocence in a child's eyes?

Can anybody dig into his pocketbook and buy a good conscience or a lifetime of proud accomplishment?

No man can trade hard cash for the companionship of a true friend nor purchase at any price the love and devotion of a good woman.

Because freedom is old, not young, yet it is born anew in the first cry of a free man's son;

It is not a living thing, yet it dies if we do not love it;

It is not weak, yet it must be defended;

It is light, yet it weighs heavy on him who is without it;

It is without price, yet it dearly costs the one who sells it;

It is not small, but great; yet once lost, it is never, never found again.

Yes, to be born free is an accident;
To live free is a responsibility;
But to die free is an obligation.

CHAPTER 2

UNCIVIL NATION: BATTLE GROUND OR COMMON GROUND?

"What do we want? Civility! When do we want it? Within a reasonable timeframe!"
— Protest sign at a Rally for Civility

How times change! Yet, they remain the same. On July 11, 1804, former Vice President Aaron Burr killed New York Federalist Alexander Hamilton in a pistol duel which took place at Weehawken, New Jersey. Such duels were generally called, "affairs of honor" and were considered a *civil* means to arbitrate long-standing disputes between two gentlemen. Americans have gone through some fairly uncivil times in our history as well as some civil periods. Although we no longer engage in duels as a solution to disagreement, we have certainly become quite uncivil in verbal communication with each other. We've also forgotten in large measure how to work with others towards similar goals. Instead, we reword these similar goals to make them suit differing ideologies and purposes. Therefore, we are more easily disposed to create disagreement and rancor from goals that should be much more universally shared and upheld. We celebrate the differences instead of recognizing the similarities. We have become a battle ground in what should be common ground.

Here's an example of battleground America. On April 1, 2016, Maine Governor Paul LePage refused to swear in a newly-elected Democrat State Senator because the Maine Legislature did not approve the Governor's pick for the Maine Unemployment Insurance Commission:

> AUGUSTA -- Gov. Paul LePage abruptly canceled a swearing-in ceremony Friday morning for a newly elected senator representing the Biddeford area in response to Democratic lawmakers' votes against one of his nominees.
>
> Sen.-elect Susan Deschambault, a Democrat who won a special election Tuesday in Senate District 32, showed up with her family at LePage's office for her scheduled swearing in at 8:50 a.m. only to be told the event had been canceled.

Democrats reacted angrily to LePage's decision, accusing the governor of petty politics and punishing members of a Senate District over an entirely unrelated issue.

"Today's decision is shameful," Senate Minority Leader Sen. Justin Alfond, D-Portland, said in a news conference. "It's disrespectful to Susan, her family and to 38,101 voters of Senate District 32. The governor is denying the people of Senate District 32 of having a voice."

Deschambault said she initially wondered whether she was the victim of an April Fool's joke when told the ceremony would not happen.

"The governor owes it to the state and owes it to a group of people in southern Maine who are waiting to have someone represent them and vote for them and their interests," Deschambault told reporters. "That's been since the end of January. It took a long time to get elected. I am here today and I am waiting and waiting, and so are the people back home." (Miller, 2016)

Much has been written about civility in our times but either no one is reading it or we are just ignoring it. It also seems to me that we are more and more short-sighted because we fail to teach and build into our youth a respect for history. Today's youth sometimes believe that the world is seeing whatever social phenomena is occurring for the very first time, just as they are seeing it for the first time. Both young and old then have a tendency to float trial balloons (try something to see what the reaction is) in response to crises and events – because they have no bedrock of knowledge to fall back on in search of other reactions.

Civility can nevertheless be practiced under such circumstances – the lack of historical knowledge or an inadequate civic grounding. It can make things work better in the New Americanism by simply taking one additional step before answering an "action with an immediate action." That step is reflection.

For example, it's uncivil to disrupt someone when that person is speaking. This includes at political rallies like the ones we see during presidential campaigns. At a recent presidential candidate's political rally, a college student stood up from her seat, moved to a nearby aisle, thrust her fist into the air and started shouting "Black lives matter" repeatedly at the top of her lungs. She was jeered by some of the crowd and soon the police removed her from the building. By her own admission she felt that she was not in control of herself, stating, "Something just took over and I was unaware of what I was doing but I did it anyway." She therefore absolved herself of the responsibility to be civil because she was not in control of herself, yet she states that she went to the rally for the express purpose of disrupting it.

There is just so much wrong with these types of actions. First, we are indeed in control of ourselves – civility demands it. If you are not in control of yourself then you are a danger to society. Second, public events are not done so as to provide protesters with a platform to lose control and promote their own beliefs and perspectives. In this case, the political rally was held to celebrate the candidate's recent victories and rally the supporters to future victories. By uncivilly disrupting that event, the screaming lady is really saying, "You do not have the right to put on this event and my aim is to deny you that right." She is also saying, "My cause is more important than yours. I have more of a right to speak at your own event than you do and I'll do that at any cost."

Consider the incivility of the District of Columbia Mayor, Muriel Bowser:

> Mayor Muriel Bowser has banned city employees from official travel to North Carolina, joining a growing list of governors and mayors who've forbidden trips to the state. The move was made because of a law signed last week by Republican Gov. Pat McCrory that requires transgender people to use public restroom facilities that

correspond with their gender at birth. The law also excludes lesbian, gay, bisexual and transgender people from statewide protections against discrimination. The law is being challenged in federal court. Bowser, a Democrat, signed an order on Thursday barring city employees from official travel to North Carolina until the law is repealed. Her order says the District government values "equal treatment for members of the LGBTQ communities (Associated Press, 2016).

What gives Mayor Bowser the right to impose these restrictions based on her own personal ideology, or what she feels is right? As Mayor, shouldn't she be more interested in the gain that Washington, D.C. could experience by exchanging best practices (widely accepted ways of solving similar challenges and problems) and other valuable information with other states? Couldn't some of those gains save lives, perhaps? We'll never know because freedoms were withdrawn strictly on the basis of ideology. This is a perversion of public service and runs contrary to the New Americanism.

Even in the rambunctious and sometimes violent 1968 Democratic National Convention in Chicago, protesters filed for and received rights to assemble at various areas around the convention site. Protesters like Abbie Hoffman, Jerry Rubin, and Dave Dellinger organized protests and brought in many protesters from all over the country during that tumultuous week. When they went beyond their approvals, the Chicago Police stepped in and removed them.

In today's seemingly — *anything goes* — culture, protesters feel that they are justified to just disrupt anything they want and that this is "free speech". This happens because some elected officials have done these things too, and have continued to lead them to believe that indeed any behavior is justifiable. All you have to do, they say, is just to claim free speech in undertaking such protests.

Stimulus and Response

Psychologist Victor Frankl once said, "Between stimulus and response there is a space. In that space is our power to choose our response. In our response lies our growth and our freedom." The protester previously mentioned obviously had no space between stimulus and response. The far more civil and reasonable approach is to have a healthy space between stimulus and response which would allow for a much more powerful and effective response.

Civility – Defined

I like the definition of civility proposed by Tomas Spath and Cassandra Dahnke, founders of the Institute for Civility in Government:

> "Civility is claiming and caring for one's identity, needs and beliefs without degrading someone else's in the process."

The concept of proper behavior has been taught to youth through the ages. Usually, the teaching is that there is a distinction between physical abuse and name-calling. "Sticks and Stones" is an English language children's rhyme, dating back to the mid-1800s:

> "Sticks and stones will break my bones but words will never harm (or hurt) me."

It persuades the victim of name-calling to ignore the taunt, to refrain from physical retaliation, and to remain calm and rational. This simple rhyme refers to our commonly accepted culture relating to civil assault. It portends that mere name-calling does not require a response action, while the use of physical force does. In our times, the "Sticks and Stones" rhyme no longer applies because in a world of instant and pervasive global communications, name-calling and other employments of incivility within public discourse can hurt a great deal. Such incivility can sway public opinion in powerful ways.

Incivility is a path to societal breakdown. Among its effects are fear in the workplace, lack of self-efficacy, paralysis of public leadership, no trust, steering the best and brightest away from politics, lack of effective communication, and more incivility

The Road to Civility in the New Americanism

We've got to find ways to reduce anonymity on the Internet – make a stand but make it yours. Anyone can mouth off with uncivil comments using a *handle* or a false identity when posting or replying to articles and content that is web-based. We must teach our children that if it's worth saying, it's worth identifying it back to you. The highest respect goes to people who don't cover their own identity. Former Attorney General of Texas John Ben Shepperd once remarked in the 1950s,

"Show me a man with no identifiable stand on a clear-cut issue, and I'll show you a man with no identifiable character or value to his community. You can try so hard to stay away from the pro and the con that you become blind to the right and the wrong."

We need more education about civic responsibilities and civics in general. This will help to raise our levels of civility with each other. This type of education is a *cradle-to-grave* process, providing low-cost, high-quality civics training as incubators of citizen planning and involvement. These should also include experiential programs, volunteering, and community service. Former school superintendent and Common Cause founder John Gardner said that community service helps "to give your life meaning and to discharge your obligation to society."

Newt Gingrich, the 50th speaker of the U.S. House of Representatives, historian, political consultant, author, and 2012 presidential candidate said about civility:

> "When I talk about civility, I don't mean avoiding conflict," Gingrich explained. "The notion of civility is in fact something we don't spend enough time on. We don't appreciate how deeply it is a part of the fabric of a free society."
>
> "Keeping passion within boundaries is vital for remaining civil in politics," Gingrich said.
>
> He added, "Everyone has a right to their own opinion. It's important to understand the opposing argument and where their perspective comes from." He explained that his words to live by are listen, learn, help and lead. "You don't know what someone is saying unless you listen," he said. "You learn when you ask questions, and you help when asked for advice. After listening, learning and helping, you will be asked to lead." For millennial voters, he advised, "You remain civil by listening to the person

you disagree with and respecting each other." (Halfacre, 2016)

Civility in Government

I saw an interesting sign the other day. It read, "Too much pluribus and not enough unum!"

Within government lies a huge opportunity for civility to flourish – if we chose to espouse it. The principles of civility in government are:

- Pre-eminence of the facts
- Respect for 1) Opponents, 2) Public Office, 3) Public
- Emphasis on policy
- Responsibility

For example, which of the following statements would you say are uncontestable facts?

- Nearly two-thirds of the latest $3.5 trillion U.S. national budget went directly to individuals as entitlement payments, such as those for Social Security, Medicare, Medicaid, food stamps, etc.
- The top 20% of taxpayers account for almost 70% of tax revenue. The Pareto Rule is apparently at work here (approximately 80% of the effects come from 20% of the causes).
- The U.S. national debt is currently over $18 trillion.

- The U.S. has one of the highest tax rates on corporations in the world.
- In 2016, a 74-year old avowed Democratic Socialist became the first non-Christian to win a presidential primary.

Answer- they are all facts. Ideology seems to bridle our willingness to acknowledge facts if they don't align with our worldviews. The New Americanism calls for a 100% respect for the facts whatever they may be and however unpleasant they may appear to us. Politicians can become statesmen by employing a total respect for the facts. They can also do so by ceasing to commit *sins of omission* – not talking about facts that don't support their views. Indeed, the first step in bringing our fractured country back together again is a mutual respect of the facts. Only by doing so can we hope for real progress.

President Reagan led the battle for civility by always reminding his team to "attack the idea but not the person". We have seen in the 2016 campaign enough examples of incivility to go around. We must not allow our children to think that such behavior is desirable – it is not. These behaviors ought to be roundly condemned by us all in our various capacities – at home, in the press, at school, and elsewhere.

To let those behaviors stand, or worse yet applaud them as appropriate, is to abdicate our civic responsibilities in the New Americanism. Every American, no matter what the political party he or she belongs to, must rise up and object to this puerile behavior loudly and often. If someone employs a very strong negative statement, that person must be prepared to cite a basis for the statement.

Civility Starts in the Home

In the New Americanism, parents teach their children at an early age to be civil and respectful to others – and to the truth. This is getting difficult in our times because of broken families and families with no set *boundaries*. When a family sets behavioral boundaries, it establishes the framework for acceptable behavior by the members of that household. Both parents and children are forbidden to transgress those boundaries and that leads to the learning of civility in a powerful way. By extension, those familial principles of behavior are then extended to a larger public audience at town halls and school meetings, for example. Children learn that it is not the person with the loudest dissenting voice that rules. Rather, it's usually the person with the most logical and convincing argument.

Our first president, George Washington, copied into his notebook 110 "rules of civility, and decent behavior in company and conversation" which he took from a 16th century French Jesuit text. Rule #

6 is: "Sleep not while others speak; sit not when others stand; speak not when you should hold your peace; walk not when others stop" (Washington, Year Unknown). Parents would do well to teach President Washington's civility lessons to their own children.

Civility in Religion

As Americans, we are very much aware that everyone has the right to choose and practice his/her own religion and that tolerance is the key. There have been several recent examples of public servants refusing to serve citizens who they feel are in contrast to their religious beliefs. This is not civil and not appropriate. Although a company can refuse to serve a customer for various reasons, it cannot refuse service to customers based on discrimination, either for sex, gender, race, color, or religion. Here's the difference: refusing to serve a customer because he has no shirt or shoes is permissible (if that's the policy) whereas refusing to serve someone who is LGBTQ because of the company's religious beliefs is against federal and sometimes state and local laws. The rule of law comes into play in that case.

We also cannot single out a certain religion and ascribe a policy that is uniquely addressed to them, such as immigration constraints or any other such deviation. This runs counter to our beliefs as Americans and is just uncivil behavior.

In other words, a president should not identify a single class of people for different treatment such as denying immigration or visitation of all people who follow the Islam religion because we are fighting radical Islam. The government can, however, stop or slow legal immigration from a particular country for other reasons and that country might have a preponderance of a certain religion. But if the government chooses to do that, it also runs the risk of covert or circuitous uncivil behavior. I'm not saying it's necessarily wrong – rather, that there is a choice involved with corresponding consequences.

Civility in Education

This is all about bullying. We cannot let this trend continue in our schools. I haven't done a statistical analysis on bulling recently but just a casual review of trends leads me to believe that we are not progressing in civility in this area. We certainly risk getting a whole lot worse with the immature primary debate behavior of the 2016 crop of presidential candidates. What do you expect from your school-age children when they see this type of behavior on their television screens? They will imitate it and bullying will get worse in our schools.

Children in their formative years are doing just that – being formed. In the New Americanism, public servants and educators demonstrate correct and appropriate behaviors so that the students can develop role models instead of being lost and socially detached in a sea of mediocrity. Their heroes need to be those who show civility and respect no matter what the situation is and no matter how hard it is to do so. Many more civil mentors and coaches are needed in our times to satisfy this great need.

Summary

The New Americanism calls for reaching common ground – not wallowing in a battle ground without progress in strengthening our republic. Former Governor Mike Huckabee has stated, "There is no marriage that works without compromise by both partners – and so it is with politics. The idea that you get everything that you want, all the time, is simply not true."

True civility requires better listening skills – active listening on our parts. Then the stimulus – response construct comes into play. We can lengthen the space between stimulus and response so that healthy reflection can take place – and that will lead to a far more civil response in most cases. Over time, these new civil behaviors will result in higher levels of trust. More trust will lead to common ground and therefore benefit every American.

CHAPTER 3

THE RISE OF THE POLITICAL PARTIES

"The media has created the perception that the voters choose [the nominee]. That's the conflict here."
— Curly Haugland, unbound GOP delegate from North Dakota

Mr. John Gardner, the founder of Common Cause in 1970 and the only Republican on President Lyndon Johnson's cabinet said, with respect to the Democratic and Republican parties: "I think of people sitting in an ancient automobile by the side of the road. The tires are flat and the drive shaft is bent, but they're engaged in a great argument as to whether they should go to Phoenix or San Francisco. In my imagination, I am standing by the road saying, `You're not going anywhere till you fix the god____ car.' The "GD" car in our times could be a euphemism for the republic. Do you think that the rise of the political parties and the ideologies pose a clear and present danger to the republic?

There are many problems associated with our political system and each of the three branches of government. For example, Ms. Janine Turner, actress and political activist, has made it her business to convince national legislators to pass legislative reforms related to reducing the size and complexity of bills. No one, including legislators, can read and understand the extremely large bills that are presented for vote. Their staffers work tirelessly to summarize those bills for them and tell them if there are any dangers lurking that might go against their party platforms or personal ideology.

Bundling is a current problem in the legislative branch. This is an exercise in consolidation; putting many small bills together as one so that smaller *earmarks* and *pork* bills can ride the coattails of larger bills that stand a very good chance of passing. When you think about it, that process is unconscionable. If you object to it, however, you risk being labeled as "naïve" or ignorant of the efficient legislative process. My belief is that bills ought to be stand-alone or at least if some measure of bundling is done, that the bills are coherent and integrated with respect to their subject matter. This would significantly benefit us by clarifying what the bill is actually about – a single idea or proposal is best. And if you must do "bundling" of bills, keep the entire package under a certain size.

In this chapter however, we will examine the role of the political parties in the presidential election process, beginning with the caucuses and primaries. We have seen in our times a definite rise in the power and influence of political parties. We have also seen a tremendous polarization of ideologies inside the parties. This is not good for the New Americanism.

The Superdelegate Super Problem

Headline: 'Sanders takes New Hampshire Primary by a landslide; Clinton Has More Delegates than Sanders!'

What kind of nonsense is this? Well, it's the kind that is seldom reported by the mainstream press. The fact that while a candidate can beat his opponent by 21 percentage points in a primary, the opponent can actually win more delegates and subsequently wind up to be that political party's eventual nominee.

How, you ask?

By the tremendous and unbridled power of the superdelegate. State delegations select the superdelegates and you can bet that there's a lot of jockeying for these highly desirable positions of influence and power. Some are celebrities, some are long-time party servants, while others are elected office holders. They are all sponsored into the superdelegate ranks by other powerful people.

Here's how the delegate situation looked after the Iowa caucus, heading into the first primary (New Hampshire):

	PLEDGED DELEGATES		SUPERDELEGATES		TOTAL	
	Clinton	Sanders	Clinton	Sanders	Clinton	Sanders
Iowa	23	21	6	0	29	21
New Hampshire	0	0	0	0	0	0
Other States	0	0	393	16	393	16
Total	23	21	399	16	422	37

Source: www.http://www.democraticconventionwatch.com/, Feb 9, 2016

So for the Democratic Party, here was the vote situation on February 9, 2016:

DEM DELEGATE COUNT

Clinton	Sanders
422	37

2382 to win

Source: www.http://www.democraticconventionwatch.com/, Feb 9, 2016

The following chart shows the Democrat superdelegate panorama in a bit more detail:

Candidate	Distinguished party leaders	Governors	Senators	Representatives	DNC members	Totals
Hilary Clinton	8	19	39	157	138	355
Bernie Sanders	1	0	1	2	10	14
Martin O'Malley	0	0	0	1	1	2
Uncommitted	11	7	7	33	283	341
Totals	20	20	47	193	432	712

Source: https://en.wikipedia.org/wiki/List_of_Democratic_Party_superdelegates,_2016

Former President Bill Clinton, for example, is a Democratic Party "Distinguished Party Leader" superdelegate, or *DPL*. Bernie Sanders is a superdelegate, as well as Andrew Cuomo, Howard Dean, Walter Mondale, Dick Durbin, Al Franken and a host of other similar personalities.

Subversion of Democratic Principles

Is this a fair and democratic way to elect a party's nominee? No, neither is it fair, nor is it ethical, and it is clearly a subversion of the *spirit* of our republic. While it's true that our government was conceived with notions of checks and balances among the branches, these notions should not extend to the *political parties*. In other words, there should never be a *check* or *balance* by a political party on the will of the people to vote for and eventually elect that party's candidate. Currently, for every real and honest vote by an American citizen, there could be many more "engineered" votes that have a nullifying effect over our sacred democratic process.

The superdelegate system is traceable to the early 1980s. Senator Walter Mondale supported these subversive manipulations brought about by the Hunt Commission and the Democratic National Committee.

The basic goal was to maintain control of the party establishment, in other words the superiority and standing of centrist candidates (the extreme leftward polarization of the party didn't come until much later). Mondale was the clear superdelegate choice in 1984 but was badly beaten by Republican Reagan in the general elections. When Jesse Jackson picked up speed and momentum in the 1988 primaries, the party machine again kicked in to ensure that no mavericks or outsiders would be allowed in the inner circle of the party. The superdelegate's votes were more than enough to ensure stopping Jackson in his tracks and ensure a party victory for Dukakis.

Mondale really believed that the superdelegate system was the way to go.

> The election is the business of the people. But the nomination is more properly the business of the parties. The problem lies in the reforms that were supposed to open the nominating process. Party leaders have lost the power to screen candidates and select a nominee. The solution is to reduce the influence of the primaries and

boost the influence of the party leaders. The superdelegate category established within the Democratic Party after 1984 allows some opportunity for this, but should be strengthened (1992).

How many Americans would agree with Mr. Mondale? Isn't the *entire* election process the business of the people as well? Shouldn't we have the most important role in deciding who the parties ratify as their eventual candidate?

If, for example, most Republicans vote in the caucuses and primaries that Donald Trump be their standard-bearer, then he should be exactly that. The Republican Party should not be allowed to subvert that process in any way. It shouldn't be allowed to *superdelegate* its way to a more "acceptable" establishment candidate. And – it doesn't. Current Republican-party processes permit the appointment of three additional persons to a state delegation after they have been selected. These individuals—who number fewer than 200—enjoy the same rights and privileges of the other delegates.

The problem with having a superdelegate wedge in the voting process is that it flies in the face of a freely-elected government by the people. The superdelegate premise is that these people know far better than we do about what's right for their party and our country; that they can thwart the natural flow because they think that the right result will not be obtained. Sounds a lot like elitism, doesn't it?

History of the Presidential Candidate Nominating Process

The U.S. Constitution does not address in any way how candidates are chosen for presidential office. Therefore, there is absolutely no basis to say that we are following the founder's intentions in producing candidates in a democratic fashion. The founders didn't envision the two-party system that we evolved into so they didn't include any language about it. The Democrats and Republicans of our times are free to select a candidate any way that they choose. Hypothetically, they could just name someone and skip all the ridiculous "debates" and voting process. Ah, but the primaries and caucuses serve to provide a rational basis for selection so that the party can generally rest assured that the candidate will have popular voting support in the general elections.

Over the years, the political parties have written the rules that prescribe their processes for selecting their standard-bearers. These rules are agreed upon and respected by the candidates so that they can't change the established process in mid-stream. In other words, party leaders can't stage a *brokered convention* at which a *nonqualified* candidate is chosen, and some *dark horse* that they name because they are disenamored with the front runners.

The Current Reality of the Party Nomination Process

We can all take heart in the fact that our presidential nominating process is more open than that of the Roman Catholic Church selecting the next Pope. But really that's not saying a whole lot. For all the weirdness though, perhaps we would be better off by doing it all in secret and then letting black or white smoke billow from the White House at the appropriate moment. Just kidding, hold your cards and letters. As we've said, "We didn't break this but we will bind together to fix it!"

The way that Americans produce a party's candidate is democratic on the frills and undemocratic at the core. We have a system of primaries to capture the popular vote but these votes are then used generally for determining how acceptable a particular candidate is. It doesn't matter all that much if a candidate "wins" a state - it really matters how many delegates he gets pledged to him in the first round. It's a very complicated system and no amount of television "talking head" simplification helps to clarify it. The reason for that is simply that some states are "winner take all" states and some are not. Also—some are geared to produce winners at the Congressional district level within a state so that just a simple plurality of votes enables a candidate to win those corresponding delegates.

The political parties have written a set of rules for the process. These rules get rewritten or changed just about every four years to suit the situation. There are no "rules about when and how to change the rules" so again, the political parties remain quite powerful in the final analysis.

Thanks to our friends at Fairvote.org, here's a by-state review of the primary structure and process:

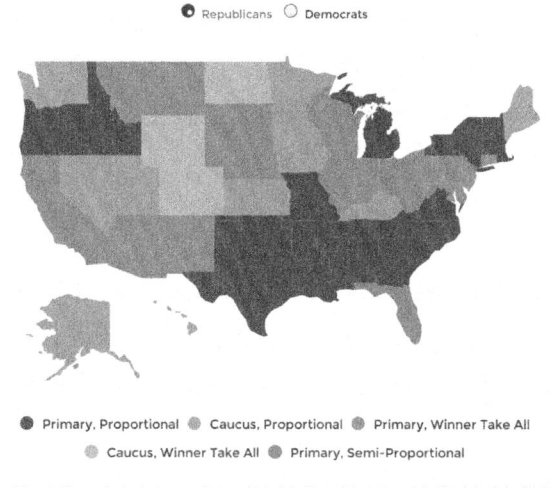

Type of Republican primary /caucus in 2016. Source: Fairvote.org

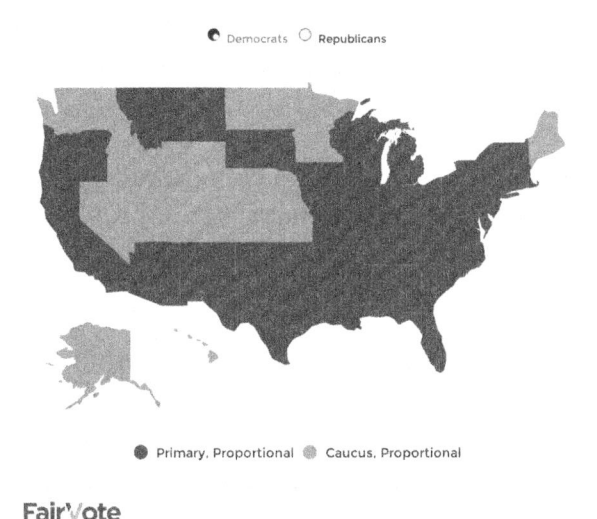

*Type of Democratic primary / caucus in 2016.
Source: Fairvote.org*

Louisiana has a primary but it is rather singular in that it occurs on the day of the presidential general elections in November. Then in December, if no candidate gets more than half of all the votes, the state has a run-off election between the top two vote-getting candidates. Some people refer to Louisiana's process as the "Cajun Primary."

In North Dakota, there doesn't appear to be much usefulness in having either a primary or caucus. For the Republican Party, all 28 of the state's delegates are *unbound* and can vote for whoever they want at July's national convention. The Democrats have a 44-page memo on how their caucus works but it may as well be reduced to one sentence: the 23 Democrat delegates (5 of which are superdelegates) will pick who they want by any means they choose.

Washington D.C. residents can vote for president and vice president. The district has three Electoral College votes. There are 20 Democrat delegates and 19 Republicans.

As mentioned previously, the Democrats employ superdelegates who comprise approximately 15% of all delegates. They are indeed *super* because they can vote for whomever they please and they can change their vote all the way up to the final moment. If, for example, a Democrat candidate suddenly picks up a groundswell of popular voter support, a superdelegate may elect to shift his/her support over to that candidate. Mostly, however, superdelegates vote from relationships and cronyism – not shifting their vote to another candidate except in extreme situations. This phenomenon resulted in denying Bernie Sanders the eventual Democratic Party nomination – in spite of his own widespread popular appeal.

The Republicans also have a kind of "superdelegate", but they are not so *super*. Perhaps we should call them "slightly more than normal delegates." These are limited to three per state and therefore amount to about 7% of the total number of delegates. All of these are members of each state's national party. In stark contrast to the Democrats' superdelegates, the Republican slightly-more-than-normal delegates must vote for the same candidate as the state has voted for. So — as the State goes, so goes the slightly-more-than-normal Republican delegate.

Presidential Candidate Selection within the New Americanism

I believe, therefore, that both parties' superdelegate systems should be dismantled leaving only pledged delegates who are apportioned by the results of the popular vote within the states' primaries.

The caucuses should also be dismantled and states' party leadership encouraged to adopt a primary voting process. Caucuses are just like *good old boy* systems that hardly reflect the will of the people. There are stories, for example, revealing that in the latest Iowa caucus, the candidate was selected on a coin toss. We can do a whole lot better than that.

All primaries should be *semi-open*, not closed. This aligns with the philosophy of voting for a person, not a party – a more democratic approach. In a semi-open primary, only unaffiliated voters can vote in either a Democrat or Republican primary. This stifles the hijinks of voters purposefully voting for a candidate in an opposing party who they think would be easy to beat. This can happen when a candidate is so strong in their own party that he/she stands a great chance of getting the party's nomination – so voters of that party may be tempted to use their primary vote to influence the other party's candidate standings.

The primacy of the states should be respected for the primary vote. In other words, delegates should be apportioned to candidates at the state level, not any level below that, such as a congressional district.

The timing of the states' primaries should be standardized. They should not take over three months to complete. Debates need to be held so that the voters can see and appreciate the differences among the candidates and then the voting should take place during the last week of that month. Political party conventions should be held about a month after the last primary voting round.

A typical presidential election year might look more like this:

> January, February and March: Issue preparation and enumeration – candidate grooming and posturing
>
> April: Debates
>
> May, June, and July: Primaries
>
> August: Party conventions

October: Presidential debates

November: Popular vote

This is the type of Americanism that is much more transparent and responsive to the people.

Because the nomination of a party's candidate is *party business* and not based on the Constitution or any other legal basis, the changes and recommendations that we would like to see in the New Americanism must come from a populist movement. Such a movement could apply enough pressure on the states and the party bosses to eventually rewrite those party rules and state laws concerning the presidential voting process.

Summary

Party officials, like elected officials, should operate in an environment of maximum visibility, clarity, and openness to the party's constituents. No more secretive engineering, no more Manchurian candidates, and no more party cronyism. At this point, I am content to borrow an often-used phrase from radio commentator Mark Levin: "That's right, I said it!"

Chapter 4

Long Live the Republic – Our Constitutional Bedrock

The Constitution is the guide which I never will abandon.

— George Washington

Many Americans do not have the necessary knowledge to describe the origins of our nation and what makes us different from many other nations in the world today. One way to ensure that you know something is to be able to teach it to someone else. Therefore, we need to find different ways in the New Americanism to learn and teach the origins of our country and the primacy of our founding documents.

If you ask Americans, and in particular younger people, what form of government we have they will generally respond "a democracy," or a "democratic government" - generally true but specifically false. The United States of America is a constitutional republic. That ignorance is resulting in all kinds of misconceptions, assumptions, and problems in our times. In the New Americanism, children will receive civic education well enough to understand where we came from, why, and what is very special about our nation.

Now face the flag, please, and let's pledge together as one:

I pledge allegiance to the Flag of the United States of America, and to the Republic for which it stands, one Nation under God, indivisible, with liberty and justice for all.

The 1954 version of our solemn pledge changed U.S. Flag Code by capitalizing the word "Nation" and inserting the two words, "under God." These changes occurred via a joint resolution of Congress. During the first half of the 1950s, several well-known groups such as the Knights of Columbus and the Daughters of the American Revolution began to insert the words, "under God" into their recitals of the pledge. Pastor George MacPherson Docherty of the New York Avenue Presbyterian Church in Washington D.C. drove the nail home though, becoming the final impetus to President Eisenhower to change the existing pledge. By invoking President Lincoln's often-employed phrase "under God" during a Church service at which President Eisenhower attended, Pastor

Docherty made the final case that Eisenhower used to influence Congress.

Despite the three additional versions of the Pledge of Allegiance since the first version appeared in 1892, the word, "Republic" exists in each one of them. That's because we may be democratic, but we are much more precisely a republic than a democracy.

Keep in mind that we, as citizens, pledge our allegiance to our own republic. That's one reason why we stand when the national anthem is played, we show other traditional forms of reverence at appropriate times in ceremonies and sporting events. It is not permissible to sit during these times as some type of misplaced protest. If you wish to protest, please examine the fascinating and admirable life of Dr. Martin Luther King. He galvanized people to protest peacefully and civilly — one of the cornerstones of our society. Dr. King stood proudly to salute our nation when the national anthem was played. He was indeed one of the greatest Americans in our history. He loved the United States — flaws and all — unconditionally. His dream was to improve it, not sit back and attack it from the *sidelines*.

The Primacy of the Constitution

The Constitution has an extremely revered place and role in our republic because it alone is the guarantor of liberty. This great document is the only thing that guarantees that the democratically elected government cannot impose a majority view on the minority. Nothing else can do that — nothing else can fulfill that role. That's why I love the Constitution – because it is the "safety net" for our freedoms and for our liberty.

The Constitution is not a "living document" as some like to claim. Those people believe that as times change, technology advances, and social conditions change, that we should just rewrite the Constitution to serve present needs. The core document, however, all seven articles, is static and quite durable. That core has been amended only 27 times since 1789 lending a huge amount of credibility to its basic core premises and assertions.

Consider this quote from the late Supreme Court Justice Scalia:

> I used to say that the Constitution is not a living document. It's dead, dead, dead. But I've gotten better. I no longer say that. The truth is that the Constitution is not one that morphs. It's an enduring Constitution, not a changing Constitution. That is what I've meant when I've said that the Constitution is dead.
> — Antonin Scalia

If we are to make America greater than it is today, and for the foreseeable future, we must return the Constitution to its rightful place – the supreme law of the land. We must also restore an early respect and love for the Constitution among young Americans. You can't really love something if you don't respect it. And you can't really respect something if you don't *really* know it. So the way forward is clearly setting about to know the Constitution, grow in respect and love for it and then defend it at all costs.

That is the process we can employ to restore the Constitution within the New Americanism:

KNOW
⬇
RESPECT
⬇
LOVE
⬇
DEFEND

Feel free to add another step in that process at the end – *teach* the Constitution. You don't have to be a Constitutional scholar to learn and re-teach Constitutional basics. After all, we are interested in the basic concepts initially, leaving the nuanced interpretations to the justices — and then respecting their decisions. That's our system. And that's why we allow our presidents to appoint our justices and get them confirmed by the Senate. This less-than-scientific process assures us the diversity of perspective so essential to our republic.

I learned all about the Declaration of Independence and the Constitution in the fourth and fifth grades in public school. I recall that the course material was called *civics* and it also included a history of the U.S. Flag and our basic responsibilities as citizens. Also, I distinctly remember becoming excited about hurrying up to be of age to vote and begin exercising all of these responsibilities.

Then in the seventh and eighth grades, I discovered through DeMolay that I could start doing a lot to serve my community and country even before I turned 18 or 21. DeMolay is all about building a young leader's character and making them better people. DeMolay claims a higher moral standard and its members are dedicated to serving others. Whether it's Demolay or some other similar organization, parents should guide their children to join such civic organizations that supplement the school district's capabilities of teaching the Constitution and civics.

Trusting the various school districts to provide a complete and powerful civics education is somewhat like believing that the police department will guarantee your personal safety at the 100% level in your community. It cannot do so. The government is certainly not an organization that will do so either. Even politicians that aspire to the highest office of the land do not understand the role of government. On March 1, 2016, otherwise known as Super Tuesday for the primary voting season, Candidate Hillary Clinton asserted, "I promise that when elected president, I will remove every barrier in your path." I'm not sure what she means by this but usually we are the only ones that remove barriers in our path – not the government. If you want a high-paying job, for example, you can remove the barrier to that job by undertaking a great education. If you want to serve others and represent them, you remove the barrier to that goal yourself by volunteering to help public servants and then running for office yourself.

Rights

It's important at this point to talk about rights because they are discussed in our founding documents. If you peruse these documents looking for either stated or somehow implied rights, you come up with at least the following:

Declaration of Independence

Remember the Declaration of Independence is basically a "divorce decree" with Great Britain but still mentions some very important rights. They are the right to Life, Liberty, and the pursuit of Happiness. These rights emanate from God, so what the document is saying is simply a reminder of that fact – not an attempt to say that man's declaration provides those rights.

The declaration goes on to say that the government exists to ensure that those rights are provided. This leads to the next right which is the right of the people to "alter or abolish it"- put in a new government that the people feel will be more likely to secure their "safety and happiness".

The last *right* in the declaration is more collective in nature in that it gives the colonies "of right" to "throw off" King George's government, to bind together and perform all tasks related to a full and free government—as free and independent states.

Constitution

For our purposes here, we will distinguish the original Constitution from its amendments. The basic, un-amended Constitution is basically a *structure and process* document, outlining how the government will work from a practical perspective. It is, however, the most important and extraordinary document that we have because it lays down the supreme law of the land. Without it, the minority has no protection from the majority – a point that has ensured our collective posterity.

Bill of Rights (first 10 amendments to the Constitution)

Here is where the concept of rights re-enters the national conversation. These are phrased in two separate ways: 1) what the government cannot do – constraints and restrictions, 2) specific rights of individuals (liberties).

Amendment I

Congress shall make no law respecting an establishment of religion, or prohibiting the free exercise thereof; or abridging the freedom of speech, or of the press; or the right of the people peaceably to assemble, and to petition the government for a redress of grievances.

Amendment II

A well-regulated militia, being necessary to the security of a free state, the right of the people to keep and bear arms, shall not be infringed.

Amendment III

No soldier shall, in time of peace be quartered in any house, without the consent of the owner, nor in time of war, but in a manner to be prescribed by law.

Amendment IV

The right of the people to be secure in their persons, houses, papers, and effects, against unreasonable searches and seizures, shall not be violated, and no warrants shall issue, but upon probable cause, supported by oath or affirmation, and particularly describing the place to be searched, and the persons or things to be seized.

Amendment V

No person shall be held to answer for a capital, or otherwise infamous crime, unless on a presentment or indictment of a grand jury, except in cases arising in the land or naval forces, or in the militia, when in actual service in time of war or public danger; nor shall any person be subject for the same offense to be twice put in jeopardy of life or limb; nor shall be compelled in any criminal case to be a witness against himself, nor be deprived of life, liberty, or property, without due process of law; nor shall private property be taken for public use, without just compensation.

Amendment VI

In all criminal prosecutions, the accused shall enjoy the right to a speedy and public trial, by an impartial jury of the state and district wherein the crime shall have been committed, which district shall have been previously ascertained by law, and to be informed of the nature and cause of the accusation; to be confronted with the witnesses against him; to have compulsory process for obtaining witnesses in his favor, and to have the assistance of counsel for his defense.

Amendment VII

In suits at common law, where the value in controversy shall exceed twenty dollars, the right of trial by jury shall be preserved, and no fact tried by a jury, shall be otherwise reexamined in any court of the United States, than according to the rules of the common law.

Amendment VIII

Excessive bail shall not be required, nor excessive fines imposed, nor cruel and unusual punishments inflicted.

Amendment IX

The enumeration in the Constitution, of certain rights, shall not be construed to deny or disparage others retained by the people.

Amendment X

The powers not delegated to the United States by the Constitution, nor prohibited by it to the states, are reserved to the states respectively, or to the people.

It should be noted that U.S. Representative James Madison proposed these changes in response to frequent complaints from the states that the Constitution offered inadequate protections from the federal government. His intent was to change the original Constitution but Connecticut's Roger Sherman insisted that the original Constitution should not be changed. Rather, it should be amended. The Congress therefore came up with 17 changes, of which the Senate approved 12 and sent them on to the States for review and approval. Ten of these were subsequently ratified by 1791 and became the *Bill of Rights*.

False Rights

Any other right that people bring up from time to time, usually to support their own notion of what's right for society, is not really a right at all – simply a desire or a want. The most prominent example of this would be universal health care, as legislated by the Affordable Care Act (ACA). Proponents of universal, government-administered health care frequently assert that it is a basic human right. In fact, it is not. Health care as we know it did not exist in Colonial times, but that doesn't mean that we simply accept it as such today. If someone wants health care to be an enumerated right, then a proposal to that end needs to be legislated and sent to the states for ratification. Presently, the Constitution is being thwarted in that way, because the will of the majority who passed the ACA is being forced on the minority who must pay fines and taxes for not participating in the program. This is exactly what the Constitution is designed to protect against – and it's what keeps us free and functioning as a republic.

Abuse of rights has become a problem in our times and is usually due to ignorance of our founding documents. For example, the right to "free speech" is cited many times as an excuse for disrupting assemblies, speeches, and other events. First amendment rights did not issue a license to ignore civility, be disruptful, or trample over other peoples' rights to peaceably enjoy the same. These behaviors could lead us to believe that these people have never read, much less understood or respected our Constitution.

Another very visible and public abuse of rights is the President Obama's frequent use of executive orders. Although in itself the use of executive orders is lawful, it becomes anti-Constitutional when it *substitutes for the legislative process*. Executive orders that affect very important and expansive elements of our society need to be legislated for sustainability. An example of such an element is immigration policy. Using executive orders to influence the fate and legal standing of approximately eleven million undocumented (illegal) immigrants is a clear abuse and subversion of the checks and balances inherent in our system. The stated reason for so doing by the president is that the Congress "won't act" and won't pass his legal agenda into law. Even if that were true, it is not a reason to abandon or thwart the Constitutional process. Imagine if the Congress did the same by saying,

"You know, it's very difficult to get the president to agree with us and sign bills into law. We think that occasionally we will just make these laws without his signature. After all, we are an equal branch of government to his."

I think you can now see that consistently using executive orders as a substitute for laws amounts to a *house of cards* that will eventually crumble and leave chaos in its wake.

As previously mentioned, the U.S. Congress certainly needs a wake-up call as to how it crafts and processes legislative bills. Many bills have become so bloated and incomprehensible that practically no one knows exactly what they are voting for. This must stop. The Congress does not have the right to intentionally complicate bills so as to fit some ideological mold. My friend Janine Turner, actress and activist for Reconstituting America, is starting a movement with a goal of reducing the size of legislative bills. She calls her proposed bill the *TRUTH Act*:

> **T**-The bills (including amendments) put forth by legislators are to be limited to single subjects, and THIRTY pages, with U.S. legal code interpretations in the side margins. An accompanying version of the bill is to be written in 5th grade reading level for easy and nationwide comprehension.
>
> **R**-The bills (and consequent amendments) are to be READ by the legislators – the new amendments are to be underlined with the old version included for clarity. They are to be available for the American people to read – at least thirty days before voting.
>
> **U**-The bills (and consequent amendments) are to be UNDERSTOOD by the legislators.
>
> **T**-Before voting on the bills, congressmen and senators are to TESTIFY under oath that they have read and understood the bills and consequent amendments to the bills.

H-The American people are to HEAR the proposed – and final – version of the bills. The bills are to be read on camera and put online so that the people may HEAR (as well as read) the bill at least 30 days before voting on the bill occurs.

Summary

As the government's powers are enumerated, so are our rights. The current confusion and legislative sclerosis in our country is in large part due to citizens, legislators, and elected office-holders running roughshod over our founding document and principles. The New Americanism calls for a renaissance in learning and teaching our nation's founding documents so that the whole system can be more efficient, relevant and responsive.

It shouldn't matter too much about who is president or who controls the houses of Congress if we respect these founding principles. The New Americanism calls for top national leadership that is well versed in Constitutionalism – something that rises above the cheaper notions of political perspectives and party affiliation. We can change party affiliation, change our minds, and our actions, but the New Americanism never changes its respect for our constitutional republic and all that it stands for.

Chapter 5

Sister Freedom and Brother Liberty

Freedom is never more than one generation away from extinction. We didn't pass it to our children in the bloodstream. It must be fought for, protected, and handed on for them to do the same.
— Ronald Reagan

Right up front we have two words that seemingly mean the same thing. Although they are often used in speeches and documents together, they, in fact, are different concepts.

Freedom

Freedom is the state of being capable of making decisions *without external control*.

Liberty

Liberty is freedom which has been granted to a people *by an external control*.

Freedom means to be free *from* something (like oppression). Liberty usually means to be free to *do* something. Our freedom and liberty are assured by the Declaration of Independence which states:

> We, therefore, the Representatives of the united States of America, in General Congress, Assembled, appealing to the Supreme Judge of the world for the rectitude of our intentions, do, in the Name, and by Authority of the good People of these Colonies, solemnly publish and declare, That these united Colonies are, and of Right ought to be Free and Independent States, that they are Absolved from all Allegiance to the British Crown, and that all political connection between them and the State of Great Britain, is and ought to be totally dissolved; and that as Free and Independent States, they have full Power to levy War, conclude Peace, contract Alliances, establish Commerce, and to do all other Acts and Things which Independent States may of right do—And for the support of this Declaration, with a firm reliance on the protection of Divine Providence, we mutually pledge to each other our Lives, our Fortunes, and our sacred Honor.

The founders created a union in which it granted liberty to its people to enjoy freedom – the natural state of human beings by the intention and design of "Divine Providence." And so it is and should continue today, 240 years later.

The New Americanism seeks to uphold the constructs of freedom and liberty because they are essential to the natural order of our society and crucial to the ability of people to seek and obtain happiness. I imagine that very few would want a state of being where people are subjugated and denied the basic liberties to undertake actions that they see as beneficial or that will improve their station in life.

Rights and Responsibilities

I discuss rights and responsibilities here because they are related to freedom and liberty.

First, as it is with freedom and liberty, you cannot have one without the other – no rights without responsibilities and vice versa. In fact, our rights are only guaranteed through the exercise of our responsibilities. That's why the New Americanism needs to be rich in both and needs to teach both to our youth. Rights and responsibilities are the individual level of application of freedom and liberty. An individual living in our country has the right and responsibility to join in the enjoyment of freedom and liberty.

To explain the seemingly never-ending conversation about rights and responsibilities, try and imagine that the structures of society are in fact more like sand castles that you build on the beach, rather than buildings or other hard structures that are difficult to modify or alter. Sand castles can be somewhat firm but incoming tides can wash them away, or some bully on the beach could approach and knock them over. They can also be rebuilt but usually in slightly different ways. That said, America goes through constant rebuilding of its "sand castle structures" of society, especially with respect to rights and responsibilities of citizens. Here's an example:

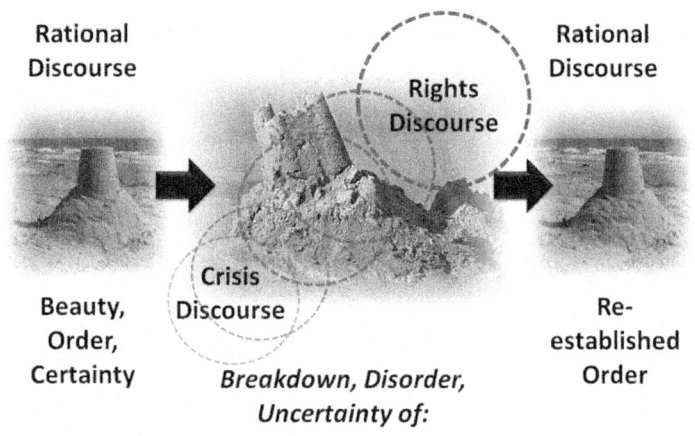

Rational Discourse → Rights Discourse / Crisis Discourse → Rational Discourse

Beauty, Order, Certainty

Breakdown, Disorder, Uncertainty of:

Re-established Order

Social assumptions, shared knowledge, shared meanings

Source: Published doctoral dissertation - Dr. Robert Brescia, 2009

Indeed, our American society seems to alternate between emphasis on rights and emphasis on responsibilities. These cycles come and go and are of undetermined duration. For example, the "beauty, order, and certainty" of the 1950s broke down in the 1960s and to a certain extent, the 1970s. It wasn't until Ronald Reagan took office in 1980 that the nation experienced a *return to greatness*. This reestablishment saw growth in our military as well as numerous other improvements in our society, all culminating in the dissolution of the Soviet Union, the fall of the Berlin Wall, and the onset of significant economic growth.

In yet another example of this alternation, in 2010 we clearly had a national discourse of crisis with a heavy emphasis on rights. In that case, the Tea Party was particularly vocal about the loss of rights that they perceived, brought about by the collectivization of America and the loss of the values related to rugged individualism. The new government administration had an agenda of "fundamental change" for the society and was doing its best to enact it. Several years later the sand castle was re-formed into one of rights discourse but this time it was primarily the liberals trying to affirm their rights to universal medical care, cell phones, and other societal outputs not mentioned or guaranteed by the Constitution. Order was reestablished along these new lines, creating a legitimation of values that previously existed on the sidelines of our society.

In 2016, we have again lapsed into the leading edge of a crisis discourse, with the sand castles of our values shifting and falling down here and there. Americans wish to reaffirm the values of freedom and liberty, and they also wish to have a livable and acceptable balance between rights and responsibilities. Any imbalance usually causes unintended circumstances and results within our society. For example, a nation that does not control its borders creates a huge imbalance between rights and responsibilities, as well as freedom and liberty.

The New Americanism seeks the reemergence of shared meanings related to social assumptions – the lack of which is crippling us along ideological lines. It calls for unfettered and clear notions of freedom and liberty that can be accepted across ideological divides. These must work as well in the cities as they do in *fly-over country* – a reference to the Heartland of America that is usually flown over on a coast-to-coast airplane trip.

The founders believed that a limited federal government was necessary to avoid getting caught in the same situation they were in with Great Britain and King George – a lack of liberty. The idea is that liberty is granted by the government and that the states enjoy the freedom that it provides. Therefore, you might say that there is an inverse relationship between the size of government and liberty – the larger the government, the less liberty it provides to everyone. While this may not be a 100% tight, lock-step correlation, I believe that more times than not, a large federal structure certainly results in less liberty for the states and citizens.

Enter the New Americanism – we wish to preserve the founders' intentions and limit the size of the federal government for some good reasons. First, the New Americanism seeks to maximize liberty and freedom – always. Second, the federal government is a resource claimant on society and should not expand past the framework envisioned by the founders. In this way, our taxes can be lower with no commensurate loss in effectiveness.

For example, a reduction in the size of the Internal Revenue Service would result in far greater freedom, liberty, and real expansion of the tax base at the same time. A significant downsizing of the Department of Education could result in more state-level liberty of choice and more effective schools within local communities.

In the New Americanism, there is at least one exception to the stated minimization of the government – and that is with respect to the Department of Defense. You will see in Chapter 7, on defense issues, why this is true. Suffice it to say here that the New Americanism needs a different type of defense, both at the national and individual level and these changes will require more resources, research and development to maintain a defensive superiority that is so great that no nation would ever contemplate offensive military actions directed at the United States.

We also need to extend a lot more resources to those that have, through their military service, defended us at great personal cost to themselves and their families—our veterans. We need a massive overhaul of the Veterans Administration that will permit many more veterans to seek and obtain medical services at local clinics and hospitals practically free of charge to them. We owe this to them because they were, are, and will be the guarantors of our liberty and freedom as a nation.

Instead of worrying how we can give free abortions to citizens, we should be concentrating on how we can take care of those that took care of us. Instead of reading articles about how adult film stars in California no longer have to wear mandatory protection, how about more articles profiling the courage of some recovering veterans and their reintegration into the community? The press and media should publish more stories about veterans' successes in the workforce and far fewer stories about the immature antics of many shallow entertainment personalities.

Will the new system be perfect? No – there's no such thing as that – but it will be one heck of a lot better than what we have currently.

Our next president must be the type of person that cares deeply about our veterans and does more than just say that. He or she will have to put teeth in those statements and the Congress must also put resources together to fund whatever it takes to accomplish the New Americanism Veterans Administration. Nothing shy of that will do.

For those who want complete freedom without any government at all, I would reply that this would surely be, in essence, a formula for complete and total anarchy. There is no freedom without liberty. Liberty grants the rights to freedom. The role of government is to protect this relationship between freedom and liberty – preserve it intact, always.

Statesman John Ben Shepperd, former Texas Attorney General, was a vociferous advocate of freedom and liberty. He insisted that good statesmanship was indeed an enabler of the preservation of our freedom and liberty as well. John Ben said the following in an address given at a chamber of commerce banquet, in Levelland, Texas, February 21, 1957:

> *We must never stand idly by and see this country lose its freedom in the name of so-called progress.*
>
> *And where do these things lead us? Why right back to ourselves. We know – if we would only be honest – that federal encroachment couldn't*

gallop so fast if there were not considerable backing down on the local level. And that the Constitution wouldn't be so badly abused in Washington if there weren't so little use of it at home. What do we need to get things back in proper proportion?

We need leaders who will put courage into state and local government by serving in office and executing policies consistent with our basic beliefs. We need business men who can use their heads to find ways of developing local resources and financing local improvements without depending on the federal government for help. When leadership in state and local government breaks down, the people are forced to vote for prosperity instead of working for it.

Too many would-be leaders will assume leadership only within the safe boundaries of non-partisan and non-controversial fields and refuse to get mixed up in politics because they think it will hurt business or antagonize the boss. Show me a man with no identifiable stand on a clear-cut issue and I'll show you a man with no identifiable character, patriotism or value to his community.

It takes a heap of living to make a house a home and it takes a heap of good citizenship to make freedom live. Where does freedom die? Freedom dies in the path over which men and women no longer walk to the polls. It dies on the courthouse lawn where they no longer attend political rallies. It expires on the concrete steps of the schoolhouse where the feet of grown people never tread. It perishes in church pews that are never filled and in homes where half the family is just sitting around waiting for the other half to get back with the car. Freedom dies wherever people are too stiff-necked to bow their heads and too weak-kneed to walk the straight line of responsibility.

We need a lot of men and women who are sold on basic American principles. We need men and women who won't sacrifice a dot or a dash in the Constitution to get a dollar sign on their personal ledger, who can take the ups and down of life without becoming so concerned with the left and the right that they forget the above and below. We need men and women who'd rather be right than be rich, who'd rather be fair than be famous, who'd rather be honest than be exalted, who'd rather be good than be clever, who'd rather be free than be secure and who'd rather die on their feet than see their fellow Texans living on their knees.

Are these old truisms too dreamy or idealistic? Will they work in 1957?

Let's stop and take stock and see if we need idealistic dreamers who recognize the need for a knowledge, love and devotion of the past. In my humble opinion, this nation needs such idealistic dreamers today more than ever before in our history! We need them as long as there are closed doors in public office, public meetings held in secret and public files marked "confidential". We need them as long as there are antiquated, harmful laws on the statue books, remaining there only because they suit somebody's political or financial convenience, and as long as there are loopholes in the law, left there by lawyer-legislators for the benefit of their private practice.

We need idealists as long as we live under big, bloated governments feeding on the lassitude of a citizenry that wants everybody to have a benefit at everybody else's expense. We need them as long as this nation is trying to live high on money borrowed from our children's unborn children. We need idealistic, courageous men and women as long as we have judges who cannot or will not lay aside their politics when they put on the judicial robes.

Summary

Both Sister Freedom and Brother Liberty are indeed cornerstones of the New Americanism. I use a little memory aid technique to quickly remember the difference between them and perhaps it will work for you too. I think of Brother Liberty as

"Big Brother" Liberty because in essence it is Big Brother Government that grants us freedom from all kinds of control. It does this by respecting and employing the supreme law of the land. I think of Sister Freedom as therefore, "Little Sister" Freedom who is always seeking the right to make more independent decisions in the home – increasing her personal freedoms.

CHAPTER 6

STATES – THE BASIC BUILDING BLOCKS OF THE NEW AMERICANISM

New York Governor Andrew Cuomo said—That those who hold conservative views on abortion, gun rights and marriage are extreme, anathema and have no place in the state - is truly a scandal. It's a scandal *if he actually thinks it*.
— Peggy Noonan, Former Speechwriter and Special Assistant to Ronald Reagan

Reserve and Preserve States' Rights

States' rights versus the Federal Government powers in American political discourse and practice—remains the continuing saga of supremacy. Any degree of historical study about the framers' perspectives on this tug-of-war reveals that for the most part, they believed in clarifying and enumerating the powers of the states and the powers of the federal government. For matters prescribed and specified by the U.S. Constitution, the federal government remains *supreme* because laws that it makes which are deemed *constitutional* have dominance over states' laws. This is to ensure hegemony and consistency for all American citizens and it is the glue that binds our culture together. Wherever and whenever there is some type of conflict between a state law and a federal law, the federal law always applies. States cannot place anything in their own constitutions that goes against a federal statute. The Constitution, and our federal laws based on it, comprise the supreme law of the land and it differentiates our federal system from a simple confederation with no inherent force.

The Feds: We're your Father and We Love You

The New Americanism certainly recognizes the U.S. Constitution's "supremacy clause" (Article VI, clause 2):

> This Constitution, and the Laws of the United States which shall be made in Pursuance thereof; and all Treaties made, or which shall be made, under the Authority of the United States, shall be the supreme Law of the Land; and the Judges in every State shall be bound thereby, anything in the Constitution or Laws of any State to the Contrary notwithstanding.

Wow! Talk about building automatic opposition between the states and the federal government. Our federal and state integrated system seems to thrive on this intrinsic tension. In fact, it is designed this way for very good reasons. We have seen that the best results for all of us generally ensue when tension is present, issues are raised into discourse, and legal challenges are pursued in the courts.

Proponents of "Father Federal Knows Best" notions about what is best for America often bring up the fact that currently there is far more interstate buying and selling so we need national guidelines for that. They also say that increasing communications and mobility cry out for top-level processes. Whether they are right or wrong is determined on a case-by-case basis. The important thing to understand is that as the nation (and world) gets flatter, the tendency or inclination to look for larger organizations and our federal government for order is apparent.

The States: We love you, too, Father Federal – sometimes

The states have reserved powers all to themselves which are not trumped by the federal government. Thanks to the framers' insistence on enumerating the powers of the federal government, the states enjoy a fair amount of autonomy that encourages us to live and work in one particular state versus another.

We often use the term *states' rights* with respect to conversations surrounding important social issues, such as racial desegregation or gay marriage. In other words, one cites states' rights if one believes that gays should not be afforded the right to marry in any of the United States. That's kind of a "We don't care if you get married in other states, just not ours" kind of argument. And by the way, if you move to our state we won't recognize that you are legally married.

Just like almost every social issue in the 1960s had something to do with the Vietnam War, nearly every contentious states' rights issue before 1865 had to do with slavery. Slavery was a galvanizing states' rights call to action and fractured the country into two separate entities. So our early history as a nation was characterized by far more emphasis on states' rights than in the 20th century. It's not surprising considering the types of issues that were prominent in U.S. national discourse. The 20th century had Americans dealing with two world wars which made us feel, think, and act much more like Americans and less like citizens from our respective states. We also faced the Communist threat of expansion, commonly referred to as the "Red Menace" in the 1950s and the race for space against the Soviets. Therefore, ideas and sentiments about centralization, federalization, and speaking with a single voice prevailed. The Vietnam War, however, brought a marked and noticeable change in those sentiments. The tremendous public outcry about the war being unjust and resistance against the draft once again helped the pendulum swing back to the pre-eminence of states' rights.

The 1980s brought about another shift back to states' rights shortly after President Ronald Reagan assumed office. He believed not only in the natural primacy of states' rights but also in limited federal government. President Reagan put most of his energy into those areas which the Constitution mandated as the purview of the government, such as the national defense. He initiated the Strategic Defense Initiative, or "Star Wars" as it was commonly referred to, in an effort to safeguard every American from incoming nuclear missiles. The Reagan administration was also influential in loosening and eliminating the "strings" attached to federal grants back to the states. This approach gained the term of "The New Federalism."

During the 1990s and 2000s, both Democrats and Republicans seemed to have renewed vigor in implementing federal solutions to social challenges of all kinds. After the Wall Street and financial market collapse in 2008, these federal tendencies got larger and stronger with the American Recovery and Reinvestment Act (ARRA) of 2009, along with Dodd-Frank legislation regulating the nation's banking system. Fast forward to 2016 — we seem to have had a resurgence of states' rights advocates. This could be in response to largely unpopular federal initiatives, mandates, and laws such as the Affordable Care Act (ACA), abortion policies, marijuana usage, death penalty, and assisted suicide.

The New Americanism also features a renewed respect, and a preference, for states' rights. Rather than make a list of all rights of states, such rights are reserved to the states *if they are not on this Article I list*:

> The Congress shall have Power To lay and collect Taxes, Duties, Imposts and Excises, to pay the Debts and provide for the common Defense and general Welfare of the United States; but all Duties, Imposts and Excises shall be uniform throughout the United States;
>
> To borrow on the credit of the United States;
>
> To regulate Commerce with foreign Nations, and among the several States, and with the Native American Tribes;
>
> To establish an uniform Rule of Naturalization, and uniform Laws on the subject of Bankruptcies throughout the United States;
>
> To coin Money, regulate the Value thereof, and of foreign Coin, and fix the Standard of Weights and Measures;

To provide for the Punishment of counterfeiting the Securities and current Coin of the United States;

To establish Post Offices and Post Roads;

To promote the Progress of Science and useful Arts, by securing for limited Times to Authors and Inventors the exclusive Right to their respective Writings and Discoveries;

To constitute Tribunals inferior to the Supreme Court;

To define and punish Piracies and Felonies committed on the high Seas, and Offenses against the Law of Nations;

To declare War, grant Letters of Marque and Reprisal, and make Rules concerning Captures on Land and Water;

To raise and support Armies, but no Appropriation of Money to that Use shall be for a longer Term than two Years;

To provide and maintain a Navy;

To make Rules for the Government and Regulation of the land and naval Forces;

To provide for calling forth the Militia to execute the Laws of the Union, suppress Insurrections and repel Invasions;

To provide for organizing, arming, and disciplining, the Militia, and for governing such Part of them as may be employed in the Service of the United States, reserving to the States respectively, the Appointment of the Officers, and the Authority of training the Militia according to the discipline prescribed by Congress;

To exercise exclusive Legislation in all Cases whatsoever, over such District (not exceeding ten Miles square) as may, by Cession of particular States, and the acceptance of Congress, become the Seat of the Government of the United States, and to exercise like Authority over all Places purchased by the Consent of the Legislature of the State in which the Same shall be, for the Erection of Forts, Magazines, Arsenals, dock-Yards, and other needful Buildings; And

To make all Laws which shall be necessary and proper for carrying into Execution the foregoing Powers, and all other Powers vested by this Constitution in the Government of the United States, or in any Department or Officer thereof.

In fact, the New Americanism calls for teaching our youth (and our politicians) the history and the way that the federal government and the states enjoy respective reserved, separate, and concurrent rights. Only by doing so will we be able equip our current and future decision makers with the right tools to adjudicate issues when collisions occur between such rights.

Texas

No discussion of states' rights would be complete without talking about Texas. So, let's look at my state of Texas. My wife and I are both Texans by choice and that's for good. I fell in love with the state when I visited it on a business trip while my wife and I were both working at the Pentagon. While we were driving around the expansive Texas landscape on the way to our destination, I promptly got lost (uh, I mean just a bit disoriented). We stopped at a small restaurant in the country, and I did something that most men dislike doing – I asked for directions. It turned out that a Texan sitting at a table knew where we wanted to go. He answered me by saying, "Well just to show you that my heart's on the right side, I'll take you right there." Casting off any anatomical notions about which side of the body a person's heart is located, we followed him to our destination and saw his friendly Texas wave in the rear window of his pickup as he peeled off, and went his own way. Now that's some hospitality. I was hooked.

We have also chosen to live here because it is a proud state with a rich tradition of freedom, liberty, and common sense. My wife and I love the people here – people of any political party, belief, or ideology. And Texas has another distinction – it had the longest period as an independent republic before joining the United States. The Republic of Texas lasted from 1836 to 1846 and had four Presidents: David G. Burnet, Sam Houston, Mirabeau B. Lamar, and Anson Jones. Texas agreed to join the U.S. in large part to relieve its substantial debt. However, it did not give away public lands within its boundaries to the US. Federal Government – just the territories which would later become parts of Colorado, Kansas, Oklahoma, New Mexico, and Wyoming.

The deal was also favorable to Texas in that it still had control over its massive oil reserves and extensive off-shore fisheries. The Texas oil reserves were later employed to fund the state's public university system. The state also had exclusive right to fish a distance of nine nautical miles off the coast instead of the usual three. This was a tremendous advantage not shared by other coastal states. It still enjoys those special rights and privileges today, thanks to Texas legislators and especially to the efforts of former Attorney General (1953-57) John Ben Shepperd.

John Ben was a great lover of Texas and he showed it in his writings:

Texans are accused of having a nasal quality of speech. If we talk through our noses, it is because we don't want to stop breathing Texas air while we talk.

Texas is so much like heaven they don't see the point in moving on – and of course, there is always the element of doubt as to which way they'd go.

In Texas everything is big, and that includes the government.

It isn't hard to describe the State of Texas – just talk about the place where people are working, praying, building, planning and growing, and bragging about it – that's Texas, and it's unconfidential (sic).

If the sacrifices look too great, remember the Alamo. If the road seems hard and rocky, and the disappointments many, remember the Alamo. And if your share of the load seems heavy, and you are looking for the help that never comes, remember the Alamo.

Texans have always felt that they know best when it comes to their state – not the federal government or other organizations. Whether we are justified and correct in our positions and assertions concerning the rights of Texas is not the point of this particular section. What is important, however, is that we have a natural inclination to fall on the side of our state and self-determination. Texans are great Americans and I'd say among the strongest advocates for the New Americanism.

Summary

The New Americanism falls on the side of states' rights as a natural and first inclination. It does so because of the clear intent of the U.S. Constitution to limit the size and power of the government to only the essentials. In other words, the burden of proof with respect to pre-eminence of law falls on the federal side, not on the states. The New Americanism also objects to any federal power grab or end run to accomplish its goals, For example, the government effectively got its wish of state conformance in an area that it had no business legislating in—the national drinking age. It did so by withholding federal transportation funds from states who would not change their laws to align with the federal proposal.

There was a kind of tongue-in-cheek 1988 movie, *The Blob*. In the movie, the offending creature started out as a small sphere and then grew in mass as it gobbled up everything in its path, rolling down the streets. That's kind of what the federal government does – gets bigger because we allow it to do so by not forcing our representatives to confront the problem. The Blob needs to shed mass, slim down, and become way more effective and far less inefficient.

CHAPTER 7

DEFENDING OURSELVES – NEW WAYS TO PROTECT AMERICANS

I will never leave a fallen comrade.
— U.S. Army Soldier's Creed

It's on many politicians' agendas and personal platform for this year's elections – how to best protect Americans from harm, both at home and abroad. What kind of collective defense structure does the nation need for our times and for the future? How can we best protect ourselves from each other when the need arises? These are tough questions but we must confront them with a bold and fresh outlook and discard some of our 20th century thinking that just doesn't address the current context – the second decade of the 21st century.

A cornerstone of the New Americanism is a shared matrix of individual and collective defense structures. In other words, Americans will assume a greater share of defending their persons at home, thus protecting the nation will be the primary job of the armed services. The collective defense will also have to be restructured around known and projected national threats rather than around the classic service components such as the Army, Navy, Air Force, Marines, etc.

The Old Days – Planning for Large-Scale Conflicts.

When I served in the military, I had occasion to read and study a document which would later be called the "Weinberger Doctrine." Casper "Cap" Weinberger was Secretary of Defense in the Reagan era (1981-89). He wrote a series of conditions which he felt needed to be met before the president and the congress could commit troops to battle or peacekeeping arrangements.

Here are those Weinberger Doctrine conditions:

1. The United States should not commit forces to combat unless the vital national interests of the United States or its allies are involved.
2. U.S. troops should only be committed wholeheartedly and with the clear intention of winning. Otherwise, troops should not be committed.
3. U.S. combat troops should be committed only with clearly defined political and mili-

tary objectives and with the capacity to accomplish those objectives.
4. The relationship between the objectives and the size and composition of the forces committed should be continually reassessed and adjusted if necessary.
5. U.S. troops should not be committed to battle without a "reasonable assurance" of the support of U.S. public opinion and Congress.
6. The commitment of U.S. troops should be considered only as a last resort.

Making a decision that is the *right* decision always includes a fair amount of taking in a lot of input, looking at priorities and ethics, as well as considering the extended impact of the decision. A good leader skillfully blends all available input information with his/her own guiding set of principles and values. In the case of the president, he or she must take into account the country's principles and values as well. If a leader tries to please all the people all the time, he will wind up pleasing no one. Leaders must act and stand by their decisions in the face of what surely will be opposition.

Consider the contrasts between the 1961 Bay of Pigs invasion and the 1962 Cuban Missile Crisis – two events that showed a maturation and learning behind President Kennedy's decision-making apparatus.

Bay of Pigs Invasion of Cuba – 1961

Source: www.history.com

In this event, presidential advisors suffered from a great deal of "groupthink", which resulted in the ill-fated decision to launch a covert invasion of Cuba with the goal of overthrowing Fidel Castro.

Castro found out about the "covert" invasion through press leaks. The ~1,400 invaders were vastly outnumbered, lacked air support and other basic items. Most surrendered and the rest died. "How could I have been so stupid?" President John F. Kennedy asked after the Bay of Pigs fiasco. He called it a "colossal mistake." It left him feeling depressed, guilty, bitter, and in tears. One historian later called the Bay of Pigs, "…one of those rare events in history — a perfect failure." Our degraded leadership and credibility led Khrushchev to conclude that he could arm Cuba with long-range nuclear missiles that could threaten the United States.

Cuban Missile Crisis – 1962

Source: www.jfklibrary.org

With respect to the 1962 Cuban Missile Crisis, the same group of advisors that were so afraid of *rocking the boat* during the Bay of Pigs event, proved to be successful in supporting an effective Presidential decision-making process. Kennedy was highly inclusive and expansive in soliciting advice and actively encouraged dissenting opinions. He used experts on Soviet culture and policy. He made a decision thirteen days after the beginning of the crisis – resisting a surgical airstrike that could have had significant collateral damage, loss of life, and subsequent retaliation.

The president was able to craft a decision that ensured U.S. goals were achieved while not provoking any retaliation by Khrushchev. He decided on a limited quarantine—only for nuclear weapons. He and his brother Robert F. Kennedy negotiated a deal that secretly removed our Jupiter missiles from Turkey. The Jupiter missile was also a medium-range ballistic missile (MRBM), capable of striking the Soviet Union from Turkey. President Kennedy also pledged that the U.S. would not invade Cuba. These actions eliminated the crisis and caused the Soviet Union to remove the missiles from Cuba shortly after the agreement was achieved.

How the New Americanism Can Confront and Win the War on Terror

Presidential leadership in our times, especially in foreign affairs crises, requires a mastery of complexity. Complexity for our purposes can be loosely defined as a context in which some controllable and many uncontrollable factors need to be taken into account when leading up to a significant decision. United States Presidents must be skilled in how to lead in a *complexity leadership context*. After all, there are many players to contend with on the presidential leadership landscape. These include their administrations and departments, such as the Departments of Defense and State, the Congress, the Senate, the homeland security architecture including the FBI, CIA, and the NSC. Every president must also consider the effects that their decisions have on foreign policy and our alliances. Most of all, they must understand and clearly assess *public opinion* and the *will of the people*.

The presidential crisis leadership process in many ways mimics a *complex adaptive system* (CAS). For example, it has the following:

- Multiple independent agents (many random variables, some building on previous variables)
- Non-linear (decision inputs come from all directions at various times)
- Recurrency (sometimes you have to revisit a part of the process based on new non-anticipated input)
- Consequence of competing factors (tug-of-war among many perspectives on the same problem)
- Emergent structure from interrelated patterns of experience, social interaction, and cognitive mechanisms (constantly morphing "soft" structure)

- Can't be reversed (random, unforeseen events make it impossible to do reverse planning and analysis)
- Needs constant energy flow (or the decision process disintegrates)

Deciding on an appropriate national response to the apparent atrocities carried out by Syrian leadership is a great example of the complexity of presidential crisis leadership. You really can't have a decision that will please everyone so at some point one has to come to a response that is largely based on analysis, but also reflects what the president believes in ethically right and congruent with the principles and values of the nation.

We will be fighting the war against terror for many years to come. As long as ISIS and similar groups have a goal of bringing about the *final conflict* between them and the civilized world, we can never rest or let down our guard. In this second decade of the 21st century, we know more about how ISIS organizes for terror and how it goes about executing its plans. We've observed and noted patterns in the enemy's behavior and how it organizes for terrorism. It's time to act more decisively on that knowledge. We have broad processes in place that allow us to restructure around the major threats that it poses—and eventually to destroy its very core.

Some politicians have called for *carpet bombing* of ISIS. That is a ludicrous proposal. One would have to carpet bomb (widespread, contiguous and indiscriminate bombing) a good part of the world because ISIS operates in cells here and there – a highly distributive network. Even their command and control systems are distributed and operate discreetly along established networks that carry normal traffic and communications. The way to fight ISIS is to also operate in stealth mode, draw them out of their *hidey holes* and then strike with tremendous and decisive power. These same politicians talk about how massive air power "won the Persian Gulf War" in 1990-91. While it is true that we inflicted a great deal of "shock and awe" on the enemy to open the conflict, it did not win the war. It was won primarily by ground forces in a carefully orchestrated joint and multinational sweep that drove the Iraqis out of Kuwait.

Some may say that such an approach is just like *whack-a-mole* arcade game where you hit a mole with a hammer – it goes down but another mole pops up in another place. While the analogy might hold water, the game version has an inexhaustible supply of reusable moles while the real world military strategy could result in far fewer moles popping up over time.

Our current military structure was built during times of conventional, large-scale conflicts – Army corps and divisions, Navy battle and carrier groups, Marine Expeditionary Forces (MEF), and Air Force wings and squadrons. While we still need a massive overmatch capacity in these type of military formations, we also need to reallocate resources into special operations. Seals, Rangers, and other task forces can quickly assemble and strike where they are needed. So we need to restructure into highly flexible, agile strike forces that can be swiftly transported and emplaced into offensive maneuvers anywhere in the world and — in very short order. Joint strike forces can take out insurgencies and localized threats with precision. They can also be used to come to the immediate aid of Americans who have been attacked or held hostage throughout the world.

These agile strike forces should be stationed throughout the world on the terrain of our allies – those who agree and visibly support our strategies as the leader of the free world. In return, they could extend coverage on a case-by-case basis to those allies, as well. After all, friends help friends when they need it. It could also put more teeth into NATO's Article 5 (collective defense, i.e. an attack on one is an attack on all). Allies could round out such forces with their own resources, both people and equipment. While the strike force closest to the calamity is mobilizing and responding to it, the second closest is preparing to support it to help seal the fate of any terrorist activity foisted against Americans. In this way, if the resistance is extraordinary, the first strike force puts it down, the second deals the final death blow and *stakes the vampire* so that it does not rise again.

The Arab world must join in the fight to abolish the threat of radical Islamic terrorism. This is absolutely essential to the success of a joint and multinational effort. They can't get a pass on it – ever. If Islam is the peace-loving, gentle religion that most Muslims claim it is, then they must show resolve of their beliefs through their actions. The world's fight against global radical Islamic terrorism will result in firm alignment of support. Either you are with us and fighting the terrorists or you are against us. There will be no middle space.

ISIL or ISIS?

ISIL, Obama's preference, stands for the "Islamic State of Iraq and *the Levant.*" The "Levant" comprises the western areas of Syria, Lebanon, and Jordan; Palestine (West Bank and Gaza Strip), Israel and Sinai (Egypt). It may also include parts of Turkey. President Obama has persisted in using the term ISIL instead of ISIS. Many think that he does so because ISIL refers to the larger geographical area affected by terrorism — not just Iraq and Syria. Others believe that he uses the term ISIL primarily because *it includes Israel*, almost as if there were some requirement to show that the Israelis are somehow in the same boat as the Arabs.

ISIS is the Islamic States in Iraq and Syria – a more contained notion of the caliphate that is growing in those areas. Nevertheless, ISIS is, by any measure, state-sponsored terrorism and we still live in a world of nation-states. The growing terrorist elements within Iraq and Syria wish to subjugate their own nations to the greater Islamic nation or caliphate, complete with a universal Sharia law system. As long as the national leadership in those countries refuses to eradicate these groups, they are engaging in state-sponsored terrorism.

Note the perhaps subtle difference between the terms ISIL and ISIS: ISIL clearly asserts that the entire nation *of* Iraq and all those in the Levant areas are terrorists by definition. Because it strictly refers to the Levant areas, it therefore excuses the leadership of Syria, for example, because only western Syria is implicated. Those who employ the term "ISIS" give no such pass to Syrian or Iraqi leadership.

Some believe that this is a calculated political ploy on the part of the president. By insisting on the term ISIL instead of ISIS, it's politically possible to give Syrian leadership a pass on responsibility to root out and destroy its terrorist factions.

Either way, we should agree on a single term so that we eliminate confusion and focus on destroying this enemy.

Five-Star Flag Officers

The New Americanism's response to the war on terror is collective, collaborative, joint, and multinational. In the New America, our smart political leaders will listen to and respect the wise counsel of our military commanders – the generals. General officers are the ones responsible to carry out political strategy. It follows, therefore, that if they have more of a say or more opportunities to influence that strategy, they will have much more buy-in when it comes time to execute the same. The rank and stature of some of these generals must be elevated both in policy and procedure. We should consider bringing back the rank of five-star general so as to accord the highest faith, trust and confidence in the brightest of our generals. These five-star generals should be the ones that have a tremendous amount of input at National Security Council meetings—and they should be afforded frequent and direct access to the president. The award of such rank should not be position-dependent but rather person-dependent. It's far more important to have onboard the right people who we can turn to for wisdom and counsel.

As with most other things that are *resource claimants*, our defense strategy must be frequently reviewed and the process to modify it *on the fly* must be made far more agile than it is currently. Again, our defense planning and budgeting cycles were established years ago in Cold War times and in many cases ill-suited to our current and projected needs. Our system works well for deliberate (strategic) planning and acquisition cycles, but still needs more flexibility with respect to being able to change appropriated funds. Therefore, we must build up enough trust with our senior generals that they may assume a much bigger role in deciding what's right for the military services.

Protecting Americans throughout the world

In the New Americanism, we never leave any American behind who needs our help. We will go to great lengths to save the lives of threatened Americans abroad and we will spare no resource to repatriate them. We won't go to great lengths to bring back military deserters or traitors, other than to bring them back for a fair and proper trial. I am not proposing anything new here. Many Americans will no doubt remember that this was a huge value of ours in the 20th century. We should not leave Americans stranded when they are in trouble elsewhere in the world. Many other countries have envied us this value and they have also seen it erode in recent times. We need to reestablish our national will and resolve around this value. We can regain our leadership position in the world by demonstrating our unrelenting will to keep Americans safe wherever they are.

I like to cite the example which was the subject of the recent Steven Spielberg movie, *Bridge of Spies*.

The movie recounts the story of a spy-prisoner exchange between the Soviets and the Americans on February 10, 1962. The lawyer, chosen as the primary negotiator took it upon himself to not only negotiate the exchange of a Russian spy for an American U2 pilot, but he enlarged the scope of the exchange to cover a student who was taken prisoner by the East Germans. He did this because he saw a window of opportunity, and believed in the American value of leaving no one behind. Almost everyone in the CIA and State Department was opposed to his insistence on bringing home the student because they thought it would ruin the efforts to retrieve the Air Force U2 pilot. He succeeded in getting both the pilot and the student back to safety in the United States.

Fast forward to our times. On September 11, 2012, our government did not respond in time to protect and extract the viciously attacked people who worked at the U.S. Consulate in Benghazi, Libya. Radical Islamic militants attacked the consulate, which resulted in the deaths of U.S. Ambassador J. Christopher Stevens and U.S. Foreign Service Information Management Officer Sean Smith. Stevens was the first U.S. Ambassador killed in the line of duty since 1979 – the same year that Americans were held hostage in Tehran, Iran. The response of the government was to fly an aerial drone over the compound and later talk about how the attack was just a demonstration against some internet video. The demonstration, it claimed, eventually got out of control and became an attack.

If you compare and contrast the two events—the spy exchange and the attack on Benghazi—you can easily see how badly we need to establish the New Americanism value of never leaving any American behind. We can't simply assume that it was too late to render assistance and write off all of the Americans in that attack. Rather, we need to immediately scramble to their assistance and show all future aggressors that we won't stand for that behavior any longer.

Opponents may take issue with this reemergence of a previous great American characteristic by saying that it's clearly not possible to protect everyone all the time everywhere in the world. Obviously, it is not possible – events will occur during which it wouldn't be possible to extract American citizens from harm's way all the time. For example, an American might get caught up in a political demonstration somewhere in another country where he could be harmed in very short order. No response could be fashioned in such a case.

I am talking about our national policy, will, and resolve to safeguard Americans to the absolute best of our ability. We can do a lot better here and we need to. We need to have the best equipment in the world, the most highly trained people to use it, and the utmost determined populace to deploy it. Much more money needs to be allocated to research and development for the kind of state-of-the-art equipment necessary to accomplish successful "strike and protect" missions.

Protecting Ourselves from Each Other at Home

We know that we have a Constitutional right via the Second Amendment to keep and bear arms for our own self-defense. This right has plenty of precedence in common law well before the U.S. Constitution was drafted. In order to bear arms, one must obviously keep them. The amendment covers both these processes. Therefore, states can have militia (National Guards who primarily work at the behest of the state's governors) and they can have armories to keep arms.

Americanism must contain and strengthen the right to protect one's self from all types of spurious attacks, whether they are home invasions, robberies, or terrorists. This is a state responsibility and the Federal Government must not abridge state's rights to enable its citizens to enjoy Second Amendment rights to the fullest extent possible.

The methods with which we bear arms are currently controversial in several states – either concealed carry or open carry. Texas, for example, recently passed an open carry law and we are now seeing Texans bearing arms in public places.

Within the New Americanism, we have a clear understanding that public institutions such as the police are generally ill-equipped to protect Americans from each other. Situations may arise and reach flash points rapidly. Thus allowing citizens to have and employ the immediate means to protect themselves from aggressors is desirable. By the time the police arrive, the perpetrator may have already inflicted grievous harm on the victim.

When I was working on the Strategic Defense Initiative as a scholar abroad in the 1980s, I often referred to a military colloquialism called, *flash-to-bang* time in my writing. In the language of nuclear explosions, the flash-to-bang time is the time measured from the initial flash of the explosion to hearing the bang afterward. We can appropriate the phrase to describe the timing dilemma in personal protection. The "flash" is the time that the crime or aggression is done, while the "bang" is the time of police response. Anything can, and often does, happen between those two times. What I am suggesting is that Americans should be able to protect themselves within the period of flash-to-bang. If they choose to do so with firearms, we should support them in that decision and have states make the processes of acquiring and employing firearms simple and clear. The New American's role is therefore expanded to accommodate personal protection in these instances.

In the New Americanism, we must also keep lawful the role of each citizen to come to the assistance of others who are threatened and aggressed, especially protecting the very young and the very old. If situations arise where a citizen decides to use a firearm against an attacker of another American in his vicinity, who may not have a firearm, then our laws must allow that to happen in an unfettered way. We could call this the "convenience store" clause because there are more and more instances in which either the convenience store cashier or a customer repels a robber and denies him completion of that heinous crime. States need to craft very clear legislation encompassing these types of situations.

Police departments already accord de facto subrogated duties to citizens through Neighborhood Watch programs around the country. They operate such programs generally by necessity. In many cases, the police departments wish to expand these programs because they are just not staffed to handle the entire workload of protecting citizens. The expansion of personal level protection in our times must be accompanied by effective training programs on the use of firearms. Everyone must go through training and retraining on the safe use of firearms, obtain permits to keep and bear them, as well as have background checks done before acquiring them. This should be an ongoing process, just like having to go back and renew your drivers license every so many years.

Most recently, police departments have been taking advantage of new social media tools designed to connect groups of people together in their own neighborhoods, such as *Nextdoor*. Nextdoor is somewhat of a "neighborhood Facebook" of sorts, helping to share timely and sometimes protective information among people in a particular neighborhood. The police are using it to share news about perpetrators only to those affected neighborhoods. They also use the tool for general public service type information. Nextdoor now has over 1500 partnerships with public agencies including 80 of the top 100 cities by population.

We should all continue to have the utmost respect for law enforcement and the primacy of the police officer when he is on the scene. We were taught as children to respect law enforcement no matter what – "Yes Sir and No Sir" were the rules. If you wanted to quibble about something that happened involving an officer of the law, you did so after the fact and usually through your parents.

The reason for according the utmost respect to police officers is because we, as Americans, have the utmost respect for the rule of law. The rule of law in this country is what separates us from those where the "rule of might" exists. At the very core of our system is the rule of law which serves as the glue for all of the institutions of our society.

We will defend and preserve the rule of law in the New Americanism.

We should strengthen the respect for the police that existed during the first half of the 20th century. If we fail to do that, very few capable and outstanding citizens will choose a policeman as a career option. There will always be police officers who exceed their roles and cause havoc in the system. However, these are the exceptions, and if more great Americans choose law enforcement careers, then the number of police officers behaving wrongly will decrease accordingly.

Will some people squeeze through the cracks in a system like this and be able to wreak havoc from time to time? Of course. No one can design a foolproof system by any means but we can sure do a lot better than we are currently doing for self-protection.

Summary.

Defense is an expansive term ranging from individuals to the entire defense of our nation, both at home and abroad. The New Americanism calls for a very strong defense that serves as a deterrent against those who would contemplate harming us. Although there are many studies of defense structure and strategy, we must never betray the basics. We have a right to be safe in our persons wherever we are – and the government has an obligation to protect us – and never leave us behind or abandoned. We have a general obligation to protect our country, serving in various capacities throughout our lives. We do this from a deep-seated respect and love for our republic.

CHAPTER 8

ETHICS – DOING THE RIGHT THING WHEN NO ONE'S LOOKING

I promise to live in a glass house with the curtains open.
— Attorney General of Texas, John Ben Shepperd, 1953

There's a recent movie and sequel called, *The Purge*. The basic assertion of *The Purge* was that people in society need one day per year where nothing is illegal - murder, rape, etc. Supposedly, this enabled them to get "it" out of their system so that they were fine, upstanding citizens the rest of the year. Although it certainly makes for great entertainment, its central premise is ethically flawed. It isn't ethical to disregard one's core beliefs once a year or to harm others in the community. It could be made legal as the movie depicts, but if you are ethical all year round, you wouldn't be able to discard or throw off your ethical foundation for a day. This goes to the essence of who we are as human beings – the age-old argument of whether we are intrinsically good or bad. The New Americanism espouses the notion that Americans are intrinsically good; we seek to do good things.

Pastor Rick Warren has stated in his book, *A Purpose Drive Life* that we are happiest when we serve others — that we have a basic human need to be of service (Warren, 2002). Most leadership theories also support that same notion, such as that of *servant leadership* where the leader is also viewed as having responsibility to serve followers, and in many cases assumes a follower role as well. Even atheists are happy to serve others. They may just disagree only as to the source of the need to serve.

There is definitely a difference between what is legal and what is ethical. Ethics refers to our foundation as individuals for what we feel is right or wrong behaviors. Good versus evil, right versus wrong, that's the stuff of ethics. Communities, states, and the nation establishes ethical behaviors for the protection of us all. Politicians, law enforcement officials, clergy, teachers, and just about any type of person that you can name can do legal things which aren't ethical. For example, a *politician* might act lawfully but a *statesman* is always both legal *and ethical*. It's important to teach our children why we do what we do for the betterment of us all – that's a big part of the New Americanism.

Public Servants – Reaching Higher Ethical Ground

There is a general litmus test for administrators regarding whether or not they would like to hear about their actions on the front page of tomorrow's newspaper. That is, a public official should gauge their decisions by how he/she would interpret the public scrutiny should his/her decision appear on the front page of the next day's newspaper. In today's world, it's even worse than the front page of the paper—it's all over social media everywhere in the world. If it would be viewed as a problem by the public, then the administrator should refrain from the action in question.

Public servants almost always exercise deliberate and full awareness of an action before they take it. If they don't, they risk running afoul of codified ethics that they must subscribe to. Public servants are subject to a series of applied ethics. The foundation of public ethics is derived from values and those values are contained within public laws. When we express ethics in words, and codes we do it usually in one of two separate ways: the first is by prescribing what not to do while the second is establishing social goals related to the happiness and well-being of everyone. Typically, these are referred to as the *low road* or the *high road*.

Ethics for the Rest of Us

We have seen why public servants have a higher code of ethics than the everyday American. But does that mean that the average American has no code of ethics – or do we have some type of a less stringent code? What shall be our moral compass – our true north?

Jacob Abbott, in his writings about American ethics, talks about how ethics are tied to American values – indeed, national values are the very source of our ethical code as Americans. Among those that he offers are truth, obedience, industry, honesty, fidelity, justice, benevolence, conscience, duty to parents, and gratitude (Abbott, 2010).

So now the way forward is becoming clearer with respect to what kind of ethics pertain in the New Americanism. If ethics are based on values, then step one is to peg the values that we can all agree to, or should agree to, as Americans. For example, Howard Schultz, the Starbucks CEO, ran an advertisement in The New York Times and The Wall Street Journal, listing some representative values that he believes should *fill up the American reservoir*, causing desirable and beneficial behaviors to take the place of negative ones.

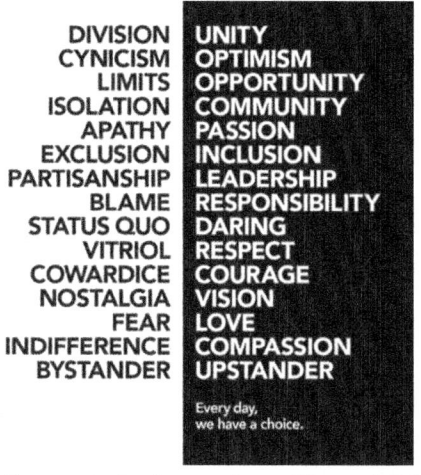

DIVISION	UNITY
CYNICISM	OPTIMISM
LIMITS	OPPORTUNITY
ISOLATION	COMMUNITY
APATHY	PASSION
EXCLUSION	INCLUSION
PARTISANSHIP	LEADERSHIP
BLAME	RESPONSIBILITY
STATUS QUO	DARING
VITRIOL	RESPECT
COWARDICE	COURAGE
NOSTALGIA	VISION
FEAR	LOVE
INDIFFERENCE	COMPASSION
BYSTANDER	UPSTANDER

Every day, we have a choice.

Source: https://news.starbucks.com/news/Howard-Schultz-on-role-and-responsibility-of-citizens

I'm not necessarily a fan of finite lists that folks tend to glom on to as the exclusive truth, but there certainly is room for improvement on the "value-visibility" void that we are experiencing today. In other words, the values expressed by both Abbott and Schultz are all great ones and fully expressive of who we can be as Americans. There are other values that pertain as well. The goal is not to have a sacred, revered, or finite list of such values but rather to enumerate some of the more important ones—the ones that we feel should be most representative of the New Americanism. As I mentioned previously, no one *owns* a specific or particular enumeration of values and principles—they have been listed, re-listed, written about and prevalent in the literature for a long time. Our problem is more about respecting many of these values every day — through our behaviors.

My New Americanism values list therefore would include:

Unity

The inclination or disposition of an American to take actions which are more likely to unite rather than divide. This includes partisan politics, the race to the extremes, and the polarization of ideology that afflicts us greatly today.

Truth

Americans may lie in their everyday lives but they tell the truth when it matters. To not respect the facts of a situation is, in reality, to lie. To hide or gloss over those parts of a truth that are hard to reveal is to lie. The first step toward civility is to have Americans from various different perspectives and worldviews agree as to what the truth is in a given situation.

Passion

Passion could include under its banner the values of optimism, opportunity, and daring — as Schultz points out. Many of us are aghast at the levels of apathy we see in our American society. Too many Americans don't vote, don't participate in local politics, are not civic-minded, don't write their Congressional representatives, don't attend rallies, lectures, or other events and just don't care about anything anymore.

Benevolence

This also covers the related Schultz values of community, inclusion, love, compassion, and *upstander*. Americans are historically one of the most benevolent people in the world. Even with year-after-year budget deficits we insist on providing foreign aid to those who really need it. We help our own at home too but not nearly enough. What has diminished though, is micro-benevolence – close neighbors helping each other through crises. If your neighbor's house needs some repairs, painting, or other things, why can't close neighbors bind together and get those thing done? In our Rotary Club, we select a house that needs these things, take a Saturday, assemble there and get them done. Benevolence requires *action* – not only words.

Leadership

Leadership can also encompass civility, respect, responsibility, and vision. How many times have you heard this during the 2016 political campaign season? "What we really need is leadership!" Real leaders can definitely help to fill the American reservoir with awareness and excitement about all the other values of the New Americanism. One of the big jobs of a New Americanism leader is to create other leaders – a multiplicity of value expansion. We need for Americans to be just that – not Democrats, Republicans, Libertarians, Socialists, or any other party - but Americans.

How Can We Bring About New Americanism Ethics?

It begins when we are very young. We must teach our children what values are and how they cannot be betrayed, or ignored at any time, or for any reason. There are many ways to teach American values. One of the ways to do that is to employ case studies and scenarios. At the John Ben Shepperd Public Leadership Institute, we use case studies to teach high school students about the value of leadership. One such study is the "case of the smoking school trustee". Basically, a trustee of an independent school district (ISD) publicly admits to recreational, frequent use of marijuana. The ISD's policy for students is a no-tolerance rule against marijuana and other drugs. When we do the case study, we divide the students up into groups. One group represents the student body, another represents the superintendent and the ISD, a third group represents the parents and the public at large, and another takes on the role of the trustees. The simulation starts with news reports about the "smoking trustee". At various intervals, meetings are held among the groups, press conferences, etc. In the final analysis, students arrive at a conclusion about whether the trustee's actions are ethical.

Parents can create "New Americanism Clubs" with school teachers, elected officials and other community members interested in ethics and values. Such clubs could establish community agendas designed to act on much of the lessons contained in this book. In essence, these clubs provide the foundations to "take it home" (put the learning into action). This has to be tackled at the community level – that's how America gets changed. Individual leaders cause action to happen, developing a following in their communities. It is essential that these clubs rise above partisan politics to the level of pure Americanism.

Social institutions such as schools and non-profits can take New Americanism on in a big way. They can publicize the message of the New Americanism in their respective classrooms and social media channels. Schools and universities can create campus clubs dedicated to the concepts.

Summary

We often say that attitudes are changed one person at a time. Ethics are a backdrop, or a *canvas* of individual behaviors. The canvas is a collective concept. Working from the top down, we can establish high-level, uncontestable values that form up the national canvas – the landscape of leadership. Good, strong national leadership can certainly help to bring these things to fruition.

Without common ethics for all of us, the New Americanism could falter. In a non-academic way, many of us need to be much more conversant about values and ethics so that we can then teach others and — pay it forward. When we can ask any American about the topmost values of our society, and we get back answers that include some of the ones we've listed here, we will be halfway there.

CHAPTER 9

SPIRITUALITY – THE SOUL OF THE NEW AMERICANISM

"The voice of the people ceases to be the voice of God when apathy reduces it to a faint whisper."
— John Ben Shepperd,
former Texas Attorney General, 1953-1957

The American Roman Catholic Church has consistently been lamenting the New Americanism. Church leaders perceive it as contrary to its beliefs. After all, the Church believes that a good government is that which helps the poor as much as possible—not to abandon the poor to do the best they can without help from the government.

As always we have two opposing perspectives of 21st century Americanism that now cry out for reconciliation and understanding. These two values are spirituality and individualism.

The Church considers it *right and just* to laud and accept the progressive liberalism that has become so pervasive in the United States today. And why not—isn't it progressive liberalism that provides for the poor by giving them things—supporting the Church's *preferential option for the poor*? Shouldn't everyone aspire to be a "big-hearted" person who cares so deeply for the poor? Isn't this why the Church supports every bit of social legislation out there that provides a hand-out to the poor as opposed to a hand-up?

Consider this Church missive about American "conceits":

> Over time many U.S. Catholics have internalized some unacceptable American conceits, like the primacy of the individual and the free market and the inherent inefficiency of government. They have come to view with suspicion mediating structures, like unions and advocacy groups that challenge America's understanding of itself or its role in the world. Counter to mainstream American culture, the church teaches that a society should be judged by how well it addresses the needs of its poor and vulnerable members. It demands a preferential option for the poor, not the Pentagon, when moral documents like the federal budget are prepared, a point frequently noted by the U.S. bishops. The church does not accept the peculiar American premise that the

poor are generally better off left to their own devices, lest their dignity be degraded by paternalism—a high-sounding slogan that can be used to abdicate collective responsibility. (Editors, 2011)

The big problem here is that the facts don't support any of these misplaced notions. Secondly, why is there an automatic opposition pair proposed by the Church: either the poor or the Pentagon? That is a most ridiculous and short-sighted assertion. I can easily sustain an argument that the federal budget is "moral" and ethical when providing for defense by citing the protection it gives to our citizens, including the poor. If we didn't have an adequate defense, poor and rich alike would succumb to external attacks in far greater numbers and our country would be fodder for the world's evilest actors. If we didn't have sufficient and strong social programs, we could ill-afford to extend a helping hand to those who need it the most. I can't think of a single conservative who would argue with that.

Both defense and social services programs account for the lion's share of the federal budget and both are absolutely necessary. Defense needs new technologies to overmatch potential adversaries. This requires research and development programs, as well as constant acquisition prowess. Social programs need to be improved constantly, kept relevant, responsive, and ready to restore human dignity and hope throughout our America.

With respect to our economy and capitalist system, conservatives generally believe in a pie that gets bigger and is limitless in size. It is classic *big pie* thinking. It's not *either – or* but rather *both – and* thinking. Many conservatives don't mind raising the minimum wage, for example. The minimum wage conversation is again lost in ideology that obfuscates its resolution. I'd love to see a Republican Congress pass a minimum wage increase! Just do it, and move on to the more complicated issues facing our society.

Liberals seems to focus more on simple redistribution of wealth – a small-pie mentality and a more narrow or simplistic approach. It is a *snapshot-deep,* or superficial view of our country's wealth. On any given day, count up all the accumulated wealth by individuals and companies present in this country and divide it up (take from the wealthier) and increase the not-so-wealthy's shares.

Civility demands an adherence to the facts – it's that which makes us civil, not lying politely. The facts are that both liberal and conservative ideologies need to reassess their platforms and policies concerning how to afford maximum opportunity to the poor among us. And the Church should be far less political and far more accepting of people who espouse both political camps.

After all, if I was a Catholic, I wouldn't want to be uncomfortable with my faith if I also was a Republican. I wouldn't want to feel unwelcome in church on Sunday. I wouldn't want to feel that because I served my country in combat that I somehow consumed resources that could have been given to the poor. Oh I know, the Church would refute that handily and assert that *all are welcome* but it may be that *some* are more welcome than *others*.

In the New Americanism, both liberals and conservatives have their feet to the fire with respect to how much they assist those that need real help in our society. The New America counts on everyone being *their brother's keeper*. This is something that made us strong as a nation and has eroded in our times. The notion of greed and personal gain at the expense of others must be replaced by notions of philanthropy, generosity, and doing what we can to help others. In this way, America will become great again – but we must start now.

American political leaders should focus more on the spiritual component of leadership in our times. This is necessary because it is exactly that component which carries the ethical essences of who we are. This is why we cannot refer to the villains of history, such as Adolph Hitler, as leaders

– because they lacked the ethical underpinnings of character and acting to improve humanity. They acted conversely, to take advantage of humanity. No matter how persuasive their leadership was, it simply was not real leadership because it was not ethical.

In the New Americanism, ethics borne from spirituality is a key feature on our social landscape. It will not matter what political party you belong to any more. Rather, it will greatly matter how you demonstrate ethical leadership in a consistent manner. In the second decade of the 21st century, the linking pin between the New Americanism's individualism and spirituality is ethics.

Ideas that relate spirituality to Americanism are hardly new but definitely worth reviewing. Here's an extract from "Americanism: The Fourth Great Western Religion" (Gelernter, 2007):

> America's Constitution forms the mind and temper of the people. It makes them feel that to comprehend their supreme instrument of government is a personal duty, incumbent on each one of them. It familiarizes them with, it attaches them by ties of pride and reverence to, those fundamental truths on which the Constitution is based.

Woodrow Wilson summarized the nearly religious undertones of Americanism:

I believe that the glory of America is that she is a great spiritual conception... the one thing that the world cannot permanently resist is the moral force of great and triumphant convictions; and America came into existence, my fellow citizens, in order to show the way to mankind in every part of the world to justice, and freedom, and liberty.

Summary

Spirituality is a cornerstone of the New Americanism – and our founding documents support this claim. First the Declaration of Independence says that, "We hold these truths to be self-evident, that all men are created equal, that they are *endowed by their Creator* with certain unalienable Rights that among these are Life, Liberty and the pursuit of Happiness." This extraordinary document finishes with, "And for the support of this Declaration, with a *firm reliance on the protection of divine Providence*, we mutually pledge to each other our Lives, our Fortunes and our sacred Honor."

Our Constitution also affirms our linkage and reliance on spirituality. Not long after the "We the People" beginning it says that the Constitution is established to "secure the *Blessings* of Liberty to ourselves and our Posterity." God is the source of such blessings, not man.

God made us all with a healthy dose of spirituality. He didn't make spirituality the exclusive purview of the liberals or of the conservatives. We, as members of society, continue to divide along these lines instead of unite. It may be our downfall – unless we embrace the combined spirituality of all of us.

CHAPTER *10*

HAVE STATESMANSHIP – WILL SERVE

The statesman's duty is to bridge the gap between his nation's experience and his vision.
— Former Secretary of State Henry A. Kissinger

The New Americanism requires viable politicians to be statesmen. For our purposes here, a statesman can be, of course, either a man or a woman. The term politician simply refers to that chosen profession – politics. So one is a politician when practicing the profession of politics.

In order to rise to the top of the politician ranks, and earn the respect of represented citizens, one must become a statesman. Being a statesman is a cornerstone of fulfilling civic responsibilities in our New Americanism.

What exactly is a statesman? Well, the short dictionary definition is "a usually wise, skilled, and respected government leader". Another definition describes a statesman as "one versed in the principles or art of government; one actively engaged in conducting the business of a government or in shaping its policies" (Dictionary.com, 2016).

We should amplify on these short definitions to describe the qualities and characteristics that statesmen demonstrate. A very good explanation of statesmanship is provided by Brett and Kate McKay:

A Bedrock of Principles

The statesman builds a platform on a foundation of firm, unchanging, fundamental truths that he believes at his very core comprises his overarching philosophy. In the face of changing times, opposition and challenges, this foundation will remain intact. A statesman may change the details of his policies and his methods, but only inasmuch as expedient tactics serve to further his bedrock principles in the long run.

A Moral Compass

A statesman does not govern by public opinion polls, but instead makes decisions by following his own moral compass that is rooted in a sense of absolute right and absolute wrong. He is not a relativist. When he believes something is wrong, he plainly says it is so and does everything in his power to fight against it. When something is right, he is willing to overcome any opposition to preserve and spread it.

The statesman is ambitious—he must be that to obtain a position of power— but there are things he simply will not do to get to the top. He is a man of integrity; he is a truth-teller. He leads by moral authority and represents all that is best in his countrymen.

A Vision

A statesman has a clear vision of what his country and his people can become. He knows where he wants to take them and what it will take to get there. Foresight is one of his most important qualities, because he must be able to recognize problems on the horizon and find solutions good for both the short term and long term. The statesman keeps in mind not only the here and now, but the world that future generations will inherit.

The Ability to Build a Consensus to Achieve that Vision

A politician may have a bedrock of principles, a moral compass and vision, but if he lacks the ability to build a consensus around them, his efforts to change policies, laws and the course of history will largely be in vain.

In enlisting others in government that serve with him to support his initiatives, he knows that their willingness to do so is based on the pressure they feel from their constituents to align themselves with the statesman's vision. Thus, success ultimately hinges on his ability to convince his country's citizens of the soundness of his philosophy.

To win their hearts, the statesman shuns media campaigns and instead harnesses the power of the written, and especially the spoken, word; he is a master orator. His lifelong study of great books and the lessons of history allow him to speak to the people with intelligent, potent, well-reasoned arguments.

Instead of tailoring his rhetoric to the public mood, he speaks to the very best that exists within people, understanding that powerful rhetoric can articulate, bring forth and activate sometimes deeply buried ideals. His authority derives from his belief in what he says. He does not make emotions soar and burn with empty promises, but instead keeps his word and does what he says he will do. (McKay, 2012)

A *moral compass* means the same thing as having ethics because ethics is all about doing the right thing. The statesman does the right thing no matter how difficult it is to defend. You may be ridiculed and criticized but you stand your ground because you believe it is the right thing to do. Acting from principle is a very important trait for a leader – and a statesman.

Statesmen are also very good at looking "over the horizon" – not just short-term as many politicians do. A statesman will always opt for what's right for future generations, not just for immediate voter gratification. A statesman also believes that he serves the state; not the other way around.

They also possess a laser-like focus on just a few overarching beliefs and principles on the major elements of civilized existence. In other words, they haven't established closed and locked positions on issues in their periphery. They simply choose the *silver bullets* and stick with them with tremendous fervor. I believe that one of the reasons that Ronald Reagan and Margaret Thatcher got along so well is that they both had a similar perspective on what was "never to be betrayed": keep government as small as possible and make it serve the people, uphold the rule of law, and keep reminding people that they are boundless in their potential.

Organizations such as The John Ben Shepperd Public Leadership Institute (www.shepperdinstitute.com) and The Claremont Institute (http://www.claremont.org/) have been emphasizing the need to teach statesmanship to young Americans so that they may instill its principles into their daily lives. The John Ben Shepperd Public Leadership Institute, for example, supplements the local school district's civics training by teaching elementary grades the basics of government, how bills become laws, and other related civics topics. It also sends up to two university students annually to The Archer Center in Washington, DC, where they serve as interns at the highest levels of government. The Claremont Institute has a series of fellowships available for young professionals that helps them better understand how to apply values and principles of statesmanship into community service.

I also add a fifth characteristic to the McKays' descriptive list and that is the quality of *civility*. A statesman is a civil individual that, if on the political attack about something, attacks the idea but never the person. The quintessential exemplar of this civil behavior was President Ronald Reagan. When I was an Olmsted Scholar in residence in France during the 1980s, I had occasion to hear Ronald

Reagan deliver speeches abroad, especially during the commemoration ceremonies of the Normandy WWII beachings. He was consistently civil and I believe gained a lot of strength and respect for it.

Stateswoman Sarah Palin explains the importance of civility this way:

> You learn civility when serving in politics at the local level. This is true because you are serving your friends, your neighbors, and your family at the local level. On a city council, for example, you are working with your friends and neighbors and whether you agree or disagree on a specific issue, at the end of the day you are still neighbors. This experience can translate into high levels of service such as state or federal. That's why I think it's so important for members of Congress and our President to have served in local government – in order to get things done for the people. (Palin, 2015)

It's the one who hollers and screams, vilifying his opponents at every turn that eventually suffers from the lack of civility. No one will trust that individual because they are too much on the defensive, waiting for that next insult or provocation. Mature statesmen and stateswomen accomplish their goals but don't resort to name-calling and insults to make their points. They operate on a much higher plane than that and serve as role models for other politicians to follow.

I believe that there are many unsung heroes who practice statesmanship at the local, regional, state, and federal levels. These super-politicians are the ones that last and prevail through crises because they don't opt for political expediency over doing the right things in a consistent manner. They don't flip-flop their positions on issues when the going gets tough. They don't pander to a certain audience when they speak, such as pretending to talk like a preacher when they are in front of a largely evangelical group. Or pretending to talk like a Southerner when delivering a speech to a southern audience. Real statesmen are themselves all the time – authentic.

You don't have to be a politician to practice statesmanship. The next time that you attend a city council meeting and sign up for your three or four minutes at the microphone to address the council on something, you can practice statesmanship. State your position civilly and why it's important to resolve for the betterment of the whole city or community. Your tone and your delivery will set the stage for the acceptance of your message.

Summary

We have enjoyed the leadership of many statesmen in our history as a nation, beginning with the first president. In the following short anecdote, we see that Washington was very conscious of his role as a statesman:

> After American independence was secured, King George III asked an American, "What will George Washington do now?" He was told, "I expect he will go back to his farm." The King commented, in frank admiration, "If he does that, he will be the greatest man on earth." And that is exactly what he did. When he finally – and reluctantly – accepted political office, he waited to be summoned by election. In statesmanship, personal self-restraint in the search for and exercise of power is a key lesson to teach (Johnson, 2007).

We've already got a lot of politicians. We need a lot more statesmen.

CHAPTER *11*

THE ART OF DISAGREEMENT – BRINGING BACK DEBATING SKILLS

When people start hurling insults at you, you know their minds are closed and there's no point in debating. You disengage yourself as quickly as possible from the situation.

— Judith Martin,
journalist commonly known as Miss Manners

I assumed the presidency of the St. Joseph Academy in Brownsville, Texas in 2009. This academy is a premier private, faith-based school in the lower Rio Grande Valley. It is truly a jewel academically and has produced many extraordinary college students and public servants. It serves a predominantly border area population, as you might imagine, being located in the southern-most city of the United States. One of the things I noticed in short order was that the students needed training in what I like to call the *art of disagreement*. They had sophisticated opinions and positions on major societal and political issues, but didn't quite know how to assertively get them across to others.

At the same time, our 7th to 12th grade students at the academy, like many youths across the nation, were being routinely exposed to all the wrong ways to disagree as shown by media outlets. We are currently in full-blown campaign season as I write this, and we are seeing some of the worst examples of how to disagree that I have seen in years. These are adults demonstrating many of the techniques of disagreement that we should avoid at all cost. We know that as a nation, we have a large problem, or gap, in communicating civilly but still assertively converse with each other.

So I started a debate team – not a debate club but a real team that could practice and then compete against other debate teams in the Rio Grande Valley and subsequently throughout Texas. I had been influenced by the fine 2007 film, *The Great Debaters*, and a lot of students admired the film too. One of the teachers had some debate experience and volunteered to get the program going. I believe their program is still going strong and doesn't cost a lot of money.

The art of debate is linked to leadership, language, rhetoric, logic, and also to negotiation skills, or *closing the deal*.

Debating is an important skill for young adults to have in the New Americanism. It can result in many beneficial things like bridging the ideological divide in the Congress, promoting and bringing about real action and progress at the local level, and opening up new associations at the individual level. It can also instill a good deal of trust at the individual level among people who distrusted each other previously. For example, two debate teams might compete against each other on a topic of local civic importance that brings the individual debaters to the point where, although they disagree with each other, they begin to feel trust in each other because they perceive that generally while the means are very different, the ultimate goal is quite similar.

During the last century, there have been periods of relatively high accomplishment in our national capability to disagree with each other civilly. These have somewhat followed social curves of stability rather than unrest. For example, the decades of the 1930s, 40s (even in spite of World War II), and 50s could be characterized by more civil disagreements than could the 1960s or 70s. The 1980s and 90s brought us back to a bit more of civil disagreement, while the first two decades of the 21st century have been just horrible in this regard. It's time to train our youth on the preferred methods of disagreement. The structure to do that is debate – we must teach and practice a whole lot more deliberate discussion skills in our times.

We strongly believe that learning the art of disagreement is best done by starting in middle school grades. That's where students begin to test their learnings and ideas in public, and with each other. It's also where they form opinions and beliefs on issues, taking from their parents' positions many times.

If you would like to set up a debate club at a school or in any other environment, there are plenty of tips on the Internet where you can get best practices and start-up experience from others. Our discussion here is to influence you to do so. If you are a youth seeking to learn debate, I encourage you to speak to your teachers and administrators about it. You won't regret getting something going.

There are many other collateral benefits to learning debate. One is the knowledge acquisition of the topics that you are debating. For example, if you are debating the relative value of nuclear energy as opposed to other forms of energy production, you will have to research and master the rudiments of the various modes of energy production. Don't forget, too, that you may be called on to represent the side of the argument which you are not really aligned with. For example, the debate could be on funding Planned Parenthood and you might be assigned to the pro-life team when you are not solidly espousing those positions. That's when your skills in debate really get tested because you are forced to argue a position that you don't really believe in. Only after you learn how to properly debate can you be assured that you will debate the position that you espouse in real life.

In addition to these benefits, students learn leadership sooner than most because it is fairly common practice to assign them roles to manage and promote the debate team. Also, the debate students attain generally higher critical thinking skills and creativity. As well, they become tuned in to their communities more than most. This is because of the subject matter of the debate – usually something of importance to the local community.

A primary benefit of debating is the practiced ability to get up and speak in front of people – something that many adults fear mightily. I learned to speak publicly by practicing and by learning through the Toastmasters and similar groups. The more I spoke publicly, the less I was intimidated by it and the more I looked forward to it. In the New Americanism, we encourage young people to learn how to speak to groups because that is necessary to practice statesmanship.

Another benefit for the debating student is meeting many other debating students at the competitions and thereby enlarging the scope of that person's circle – employing the power of acquaintance.

Educational Benefits of Debate

It's clear that learning to properly debate in a logical way, whether it's the formal and classic *Lincoln-Douglas* style or not, leads to higher scholastic achievement. There's evidence to support this claim:

> Debaters overall are 3.1 times more likely to graduate from high school, no matter which risk group. Importantly, the impact of debate was greatest for those in the highest risk group. For high-risk students, 72% of debaters graduated, versus only 43% of non-debaters in that risk group (New Research Confirms the Power of Debate to Change Lives, 2016).

Now you don't have to be a "smarty-pants" or some brilliant genius to do well at debate. Rather, you just need to work hard at it and learn the techniques. In 2015, Harvard's debate team lost a match to prison inmates at the Eastern New York Correctional Facility in New York State. The three inmates who beat the Harvard team were in prison for violent crimes. Alex Hall, a 31-year-old from Manhattan convicted of manslaughter said, "We might not be as naturally rhetorically gifted, but we work really hard" (Syrmopoulos, 2015).

Summary

The ability to disagree without venom or demonizing an opponent touches on many areas of the New Americanism, such as civility. Debating skills must be learned early on and are as important as learning English and mathematics. We should welcome debate because it normally brings about a much richer result in policy and trust. It improves our active listening and communications skills as well.

CHAPTER 12

TAKING CARE OF OUR ELDERLY – IT'S AN AMERICAN THING.

It was once said that the moral test of government is how that government treats those who are in the dawn of life, the children; those who are in the twilight of life, the elderly; and those who are in the shadows of life, the sick, the needy and the handicapped.

— Hubert H. Humphrey

This is a very large cornerstone of the New Americanism because we have developed into a society that gives as much lip service to the well-being of our elderly as we give to our military veterans – and that's not good. It seems like in the vibrancy and energetic frenzy of youth that we forget about the folks who gave us life, nurtured us throughout our growing years, and provided for us in many different ways. We owe them the respect and love that they deserve. It's the right thing to do.

Taking care of the aged in society is definitely not new – it just seems that we need to elevate it to a new height in our New Americanism. We have let it go, and it is a terrible thing to see. Bones of 500,000 year-old humans have been discovered now and then by archaeologists in specific conditions indicating that people helped their elderly even in those early societies. For example, their bones were found in ways that suggest they could not have been ambulatory. Others must have helped them to survive. In ancient Athens, it was a crime not to take care of one's parents, with the punishment being loss of citizenship.

Although one single anecdote does not prove that we are experiencing an epidemic of elderly-abuse, this incident is particularly heinous. The Dallas Morning News reported that the owner of a Frisco, Texas healthcare clinic that catered to the elderly apparently ordered his medical staff to euthanize patients with massive overdoses of morphine and other drugs so that they would "die quicker":

> The owner of a Frisco medical company regularly directed nurses to overdose hospice patients with drugs such as morphine to speed up their deaths and maximize profits and sent text messages like, "You need to make this patient go bye-

bye," an FBI agent wrote in an affidavit for a search warrant obtained by NBC 5.

According to state records, the executive founded the company in July 2012. The investigation revealed that "as part of this scheme, the owner, who has no medical training or licenses, would direct his employed nurses to overdose hospice patients with palliative medications such as morphine to hasten death, and thereby minimize its [paybacks] under the cap."

He also told other health care executives over a lunch meeting that he wanted to "find patients who would die within 24 hours," and made comments like, "if this f— would just die," an FBI agent wrote in the warrant. (Knodel, 2016)

There should be relatively little mercy shown to this CEO should he be found subsequently guilty of these hideous acts against humanity.

As baby boomers continue to age, states are exceedingly worried about their ability to foot the bill for Medicaid programs:

> The federal government is pushing states to keep more low-income seniors out of nursing homes and instead, enroll them in home and community-based programs. The shift comes as demand for long-term care is

rising. By 2050, the number of people older than 85 is expected to triple to more than 18 million. Advocates say programs for seniors often wind up on the chopping block. The cornerstone of home and community-based programs is personal care services, such as providing an aide who helps with cooking and cleaning. Those services cost a fraction of nursing home care. (Press, 2016)

Our Nation's Elderly Have Achieved Invisibility

Our aging parents and citizens should not be considered as *throwaways* once they reach retirement age. We are all made to enjoy a full life with all of its seasons. Already it seems that we are in fact *discarding* the elderly in many ways, and that trend is alarming. It could eventually bring down our entire system. If you are generally 60 years old or older, you already know that many youths and middle aged people walk right past you as if you were invisible. These same people don't greet you when they encounter you, as they would a younger person. It's a common but cruel joke among the over-60 crowd: "Oh, there I go, I obviously just became invisible again."

Almost 40% of Americans are now providing some type of at-home medical care for an aging family member (Press, 2016). This will increase as the baby boomers approach the fall and winter of their lives. If the economy also goes from bad to worse, it could create many more caregivers throughout the nation.

In the 1970s, when I was a young Army soldier serving in Germany, a friend and I would regularly come to the assistance of an elderly German couple who lived in downtown Karlsruhe at the very top floor of a large apartment building. We would go over there and carry wood from the basement to the top floor so that they could burn it in their fireplace and keep warm. I soon came to realize that if we had not done that, this couple probably would have expired by the lack of adequate warmth. It was a great lesson to me. Ever since that time, I became very focused on how Americans take care of their aging parents and grandparents – or not.

Avenues of Approach – Courses of Action

There are many ways that we can reverse our current course of not taking sufficient care of the elderly.

Help them stay healthy

It goes without saying that elderly need a lot more health services on a regular basis as the body begins to function less effectively. However, with the right amount of health care, both preventive and remedial, we can age gracefully and enjoy a higher quality of living for a longer time. Yes, there will always be calamities that cause premature death, such as cancers and other life-threatening maladies. That should not deter us from helping the elderly much better than we do now.

I propose a health care system that creates scaled benefits – mostly in favor of the elderly. In other words, the elderly should pay lower deductibles and less out-of-pocket cost than youth. This is not a plug for the Affordable Care Act (ACA). That legislation is relatively new and doesn't really do what I am suggesting. The primary goal of the ACA was to provide universal health care, not to reform the cost of health services, quality of providers, or any other factors. It will probably go through numerous revisions and changes before it can "pass muster". Public and private health plans alike should be changed to provide more "pre-paid" services for the elderly under most conditions and circumstances. The young should take heart and rejoice in these recommendations as well, knowing how well they will be taken care of in later life.

Falls and broken bones are the plague of the aged. They know to be very careful because a simple fall can bring about trauma, and in some cases death. A lot of these falls can be preventable with the right type of care and living conditions. Exercise and supplements are essential in these cases so we must have ready-made exercise programs that the elderly can follow, and more pervasive access to vitamins and supplements that can help to keep their bone structure as healthy and strong as possible.

Instead of taxing those who do not participate in health care, the proposed system would be totally voluntary.

Increased Competition to Help Reduce Health Care Costs

By the same token, we can control health care costs by beefing up tort reform and significantly decreasing the number and dollar amount of lawsuits against medical providers. We also need to increase the supply of health care providers, specifically doctors who can entertain practices that cater to the elderly. This means the return to "house calls" – generalists who specialize in displacing to the patient's home to provide both diagnosis and minor treatment. Drugstores that deliver prescriptions could be very useful to the aged.

One of the worst signs of the times that I have seen is the emergence and popularity of the reverse mortgage. This is where an elderly person can use the equity in his home basically for living expenses and in some cases, the ability to stay in the house altogether. The idea is that the equity is "paid out" monthly. When the person dies, the house generally needs to be sold by the heirs so as to pay back the loan which came due at that point.

I believe that the reverse mortgage mechanism is a product of our bad economic times. It is not the normal flow of accumulated wealth in life. Parents should build equity and then transfer it upon their deaths to their sons and daughters – not to the bank. Americans believe in the dream of home ownership, not paying a new type of "rent" to banks to be able to live in a house that you have already bought. This seems to be just another way to saddle more debt to the successive generation. They already have the national debt to worry about and solve as well as student debt. Now they will have a much harder time owning their own home.

Someone told me just the other day that young people have accepted the fact of not being able to own their own home. Some claim that this is the new normal. That's a load of crap. Home ownership is one of our most valued treasures as a society no matter how humble the home might be. It beats renting every time. Many young people yearn for home ownership and we should not make it harder for them to own one. If we age and we can't afford our home anymore then we need to downsize into an affordable arrangement – not incur more debt to in-effect live beyond our means.

Make it Much Easier to Communicate with Them

If we make it much easier for the elderly to communicate with their families, they will live longer and enjoy a higher quality of life. They may even require fewer medical services as a result.

Here's an idea: how about making it desirable for all of us of to provide the elderly with a solid means of communication. Provide a tax deduction for doing so. Do they need one of those push button *call for help* devices to hang around their neck? Again, provide an incentive for adult taxpayers to provide them with one including monitoring charges. Do they need Internet connectivity? Let's incentivize Americans to provide that for them. After all, they have a lot more time on their hands and they could really benefit from ordering things from internet websites because they can't displace too readily to buy them from store shelves. Many assisted and semi-assisted living facilities now have common areas in which internet terminals could be installed much the same as a hotel has a business center for travelers to use. Many more of these facilities could sport such amenities if they were properly incentivized and persuaded to do so.

Incentives are a good way for us to help those who need it the most, at a cost that would be far less than the cost of treating that person for some type of medical calamity that could have been avoided. In other words, a personal tax incentive is a lot more affordable for the government than some large, bloated program or mandate. It's more effective, too. Abuses will occur just the same way that they occur for any social system, but Americans are generally honest people. The number of abuses will be minimal and controllable. Many communities already run electronic bulletin boards. The identification of an elderly person that you could help could be done through such exchanges, if properly protected and managed.

I am very glad that I can reach out to my 94-year old mom for telephone chats. She lives in Connecticut — obviously too far from Texas to have frequent family visits. I salute my younger brother Andy for taking care of her because he lives in near proximity. Without Andy's constant assistance and caring, Mom may have had a calamity from which she could not have recovered. Andy, my wife and I all believe that Mom often needs a reasonable amount of prodding to eat responsibly and get enough nutrients. We send her nutritional drinks that are shipped to her regularly, of which she says she enjoys – no prep required and she gets the nutrients. We can't get her to do emails, but at least we can speak with her on the phone whenever possible. If an inventor could come up with a device that 94 year-olds could easily do email, send photos, and check social media websites, we would be very grateful!

If the young people feel plugged in when they are connected to Wi-Fi and Internet sources, why would it be any different for the elderly? We need to get creative and find ways to enable them to connect with the world so that they feel plugged in too. They will also feel more useful to society instead of just being "invisible". Feelings of detachment can bring about illnesses and have deleterious effects on their overall attitudes.

Ask the Elderly to Teach Americanism

There are so many senior citizens who have amassed a great deal of wisdom throughout their lives. They long to be involved again in civic matters and education. The rapid growth in seniors returning to college campuses for adult education courses (with no degrees, and no tests) is significant. There is a tremendous and relatively untapped wealth of *elderly energy* just waiting to be called on. Remember, elderly don't normally jump up and say, "Put me in, coach!" You have to present ideas to them first, and let them pick the ones they would like to develop. But once they are committed, they really are in the game. This is because of the values that they grew up with — follow-through and commitment.

My Grandson's Thoughts

Christian Harvey is 15 years old and now has become the man of his house. Last year, his dad passed away from a very aggressive cancer, leaving behind his mom and three sisters. I asked Christian to "beta-read" this chapter about the elderly in the New Americanism. This is what he wrote about it:

> I, too, feel that as Americans, we need to treat the elders better. I also agree that the elders should teach us about Americanism. Maybe that way it will break the gap between "young'uns" and "oldies", and influence us young'uns to treat elders better.

Summary

The elderly have so much to offer us – if we would only take better care of them and involve them more in business, culture, community, and other essential parts of our New Americanism society. Want to make America great again? Start by getting creative. For example, I have in mind a "Task Force Boomer" initiative. It could be a joint public-private initiative that, once created, might make a huge impact on many of our revered elderly.

Starbucks CEO Howard Schultz recently talked about a "different story of America" than the one we see every day. He said that this different story lives in many places throughout our nation. It lives in the "nurse who treats the elderly with dignity." (Schultz, 2016)

Chapter 13

The Truth about Youth.

Older men declare war. But it is the youth that must fight and die.
— Herbert Hoover

George Washington, as a boy, was ignorant of the commonest accomplishments of youth. He could not even lie.
— Mark Twain

Our youthful Americans have much to be excited about in the New Americanism. Both the Millennials (those reaching young adulthood at around the year 2000) and Generation X (those born between 1965 and 1980) have many opportunities to restore greatness to the nation. Take heart, young Americans – we are going to discuss some of those ways in this chapter. Although presently youth may see opportunities as constraints and burdens, they are the ones who can and will bring about sustainable, positive progress in the New

Americanism. And we are counting on them to do so.

But are the *young'uns* wilting from the task?

Claire Fox, from the UK-based Institute of Ideas, has penned a scathing critique of what she calls, "Generation Snowflake" – a new generation of hyper-sensitive, thin-skinned, fragile youth that just can't bear the thought of anything that might offend them. She claims, for example, that Oxford Law students are routinely warned when course matter "might upset them". Snowflakes cringe and gasp when someone voices an opinion contrary to their own, a dissenting worldview. They don't seem to be able to deal with controversy. When faced with contrarian views, they howl loudly in disbelief that they should be forced to even hear such differing viewpoints.

The Sun's article on Fox's research further states that:

> This hyper-sensitivity has prompted the University of East Anglia to outlaw sombreros in a Mexican restaurant and caused the National Union of Students to ban clapping as "as it might trigger trauma", asking youngsters to use "jazz hands" instead. Books containing troublesome material are now slapped with "trigger warnings", whilst universities and student unions are declared "safe spaces"

where young people should not have to encounter anything they disagree with {The Sun, 2016}.

Here in America, many have also expressed a fair amount of angst about youth in our times. For example, it's alleged that:

> They spend too much time on their cell phones.
> They are ignorant of life skills, and not properly educated.
> They can't carry on a meaningful conversation.
> They never look you in the eyes, and don't make a solid personal connection.
> They prefer video or audio teleconferences rather than face-to-face meetings.
> They simply adore social media and while away the hours in that space.
> They aren't rugged individualists, but more like sheep that seek to copy and imitate others.
> They are like lemmings who follow false exemplars wherever they lead them.
> They just don't care about what's important in life.
> They have abandoned the American Dream of greatness now and in our future.
> They are only interested in how many "likes" they get on Facebook.

They never read books or articles because their attention span is too short.

Well, this is a fairly large condemnation of youth coming primarily from a subsection of my own generation - baby boomers (those born between 1946 and 1964). Some of the "silents" (those born before 1946) also share a certain level of bewilderment about today's youth. If we spent half as much time discovering how we could enfranchise today's youth as we do lambasting them for not apparently espousing our values, we would be wildly successful in the New Americanism.

The New Americanism calls for all of us to communicate powerfully with youth and help them to solve the problems that we have created and of which they are inheriting. Don't misunderstand. I'm not blaming mid-lifers or baby boomers for all of our current ills in society. I am, however, stating the obvious fact that youth didn't create this situation – we did. But together with them, we will fix it. One of the great tenets of leadership that I've learned is that a leader should always concentrate more on fixing things that are broken rather than spending a great deal of time affixing blame. We just want to set upright again that which has fallen. And in so doing, we emplace trust in every stakeholder – not fear.

The *greatest generation*, those *silents* who were adults at the outset of World War II – and generally fought in that war—were stage-setters. They set a magnificent stage for us to develop in, leaving a legacy of greatness for us to nurture. My dad returned from serving four years in the war and went to work in a factory making belt buckles for a living. He bought a home and created our family – my two brothers and me. Later, he used his technical prowess and skills to become an assembly line tester of jet engines at the Pratt & Whitney Company. I believe that he achieved the American Dream of individual freedoms, liberty, and home ownership.

If the important values and principles of our American society are not effectively passed down from one generation to another, we can experience a rift in our ability to be great at home and on the world stage. This has happened several times in our U.S. history. One such rift occurred in the mid-1960s when we saw the younger generation *dropping out* – indeed relishing a sense of social alienation as a badge of honor. Of course, many of these same "hippies" later became today's baby boomers who are concerned with our youth. It's a natural phenomenon as we all know.

Pew Research has done quite a lot of study and surveying of millennials – not surprising because millennials have surpassed Generation X as the dominant generation in the workforce. Some of

Pew's findings are very interesting. For example, millennials tend to have more-positive views than the older generations about small and large businesses, financial institutions and labor unions:

> Banks and financial institutions continue to be viewed more negatively than positively among adults overall (47% vs. 40%), yet nearly twice as many as in 2010 now say they have a positive impact (40% today, 22% then). And these more-positive impressions are seen across generations: Five years ago, just 35% of millennials said banks had a positive impact on the nation; today 45% say this. Evaluations of large corporations have similarly improved among millennials, though they also remain more negative than positive.
>
> Small businesses were viewed positively by majorities across all generations in 2010, and those views have only grown more positive in recent years. For instance, 86% of millennials now say small businesses have a positive effect, up 15 points since 2010.
>
> Labor unions are also seen more positively today than they were five years ago (45% now say they have a positive impact on the country, up from 32% in 2010). And millennials remain much more likely than their elders, especially members of the

silent generation, to view unions positively: More than half (57%) of millennials say this, compared with 42% of Gen Xers, 41% of baby boomers and just 28% of silents.

Millennials also have more positive views of colleges and universities than those in older generations. Nearly three-quarters of millennials (73%) say colleges and universities have a positive impact, compared with 64% of Generation Xers, 59% of boomers and just 51% of silents.

And although technology companies are widely seen as having a positive impact on the country, a generation gap does exist: 77% of millennials and nearly as many Xers (73%) and boomers (70%) say this, compared with a smaller majority of silents (59%).

While about half of Americans (48%) view the energy industry as having a positive impact on the country, this view is somewhat more common among those in younger generations than older: 54% of millennials and 52% of Xers say this, compared with just 42% of boomers and 35% of silents. (Fingerhut, 2015)

So let's see what we can do to enfranchise and empower today's youth – get them going on the path to greatness in the New Americanism. Basically, I think it entails a three-step approach. Then we can be every bit the "stage setters" as the greatest generation was.

First Step – Stop the Blame Game and Start Cherishing Youth

If youth is "guilty" of any of the things previously ascribed to it, then it is simply because we have not taught them properly or there are other forces at work in our times that are very different than in preceding generations. Personally, I believe it's a little of both.

The alienation of today's youth is much the same phenomenon of the alienation of our returning military veterans. We greet veterans at the airport (sometimes), say nice things, but when the dust settles, they are on their own to *figure it out*. With respect to youth, we say nice things about them (sometimes) and then when the dust settles, we leave them to their own devices and tell them "good luck" or "See ya - wouldn't want to be ya." It's kind of a "Deal with it – our generation had to, now it's your turn" perspective. While that may be true, we need to break the chain of blame and abandonment, jump in the game, listen to what youth has to say and be part of the solutions – together with them.

Youth operates in an incredibly complex world with many more independent variables than controllable ones. Yes, they spend time on their phones – to keep abreast of rapid developments that affect their lives on a daily basis. They get their news from phones and they communicate with others on them too. They exchange ideas and get feedback on them, too. The world's "clock speed" is a heck of a lot faster than it was in the 1950s – and that requires means to keep up with it. A phone is no longer a luxury or a mere distraction. It is a personal PC that is with you constantly with *apps* that sometimes defy the imagination.

Still not convinced? Just look at what youth has to face today:

TODAY'S YOUTH	1950s YOUTH
Nuclear Threat	Nuclear Threat
Communist Threat	Communist Threat
Technology Explosion	
Global Unrest / Terrorism	
Social Change	
National Debt	
Student Debt	
Climate Change	
Uncivil Behavior	

These extraordinary challenges weigh heavily on youth as a backdrop for their actions and responses.

I interact with our American youth almost every single day and can tell you that almost all of them are very interested in making things better, experiencing success, and bringing about a sturdy platform for their future children and families. They care. They are a younger version of us. They want to become great Americans.

Second Step – Teach Your Children Well

In the New Americanism, the *passing down of values* process is deliberate – not automatic or assumed. I make this important point because the inculcation, or assimilation, of values by a successive generation is a process that requires active, specific teaching and learning. Only after that can these values experience what is known as *legitimation* – the process of entering into a large part of our society.

Who can teach youth these values? The answer is a wide variety of members of the preceding generation – schoolteachers, parents, mentors, pastors, and many others. In my day, we had civic organizations that were extremely active in teaching American values to youth. Among them were the JayCees (Junior Chambers), DeMolay (youth branch of the Masons), the American Legion, the Boy Scouts of America, Girl Scouts of America, and many others.

In Texas, state leadership decided that it wished to institutionalize the teaching of leadership, values of service to community, and ethics to its youth throughout every area of the state. In 1995, it founded the John Ben Shepperd Public Leadership Institute whose mission continues today. The John Ben Shepperd Public Leadership Institute, named after one of Texas' heroes, former Attorney General John Ben Shepperd, delivers free values and principles education to many Texas schoolchildren and college students – free of charge. In 2014, it taught basic civics, such as how bills become laws and the three branches of government, to thousands of 3rd and 4th graders.

The John Ben Shepperd Public Leadership Institute is all about youth – educating them, cultivating them, and getting them ready to serve their state in the fullest measure. It extends way beyond partisanship – it operates at the higher level of Americanism and encourages others to be at that level as well. John Ben Shepperd was a fierce advocate for the civic engagement of youth early in their lives – helping the values transfer process to become strong and effective. For example, he delivered the following remarks at an Education for Citizenship Conference for East Texas High School Seniors at Baylor University, Waco, Texas, March 2, 1951. Mr. Shepperd originated the idea for the annual Citizenship Conferences conducted by the East Texas Chamber of Commerce:

I'm not surprised if there is, in many of you, a strong feeling of criticism toward the older generation — criticism of the condition in which your heritage is being handed down to you. How would you feel if your father gave you a new convertible for graduation, and gave you the mortgage with it — with the first payment already due? That's the way you're getting your Freedom. Liberty is always bought on an installment basis, and every generation has to make a payment. It was by sorrow, sacrifice and blood that your fathers and mothers were able to give you this heritage at all, and your debt of gratitude is great. But it is not a perfect gift, and since the job of preserving it and making it better will be largely yours, I'd like to point out a few of its faults and make a few suggestions about what you can begin doing right now to keep Democracy on its feet — to insure our future freedom. One of the fallacies of our system today is that the public, your elders, and you yourselves seem to think you have nothing to do with politics and government until you reach voting age; but how can you vote at 21 if you have not prepared for it? You don't become a responsible, self-governing citizen overnight. You work at it. You study it. As junior citizens, you are now in the preparation stage for what you will be when you are 21. What you will do then is being determined today! It is ridiculous to think that you could jump into a car and start racing through the streets without first learning how to drive — you have to be taught to drive — or swim — or fly; and learning to vote takes even more thought, and study and preparation. It's not easy — begin now as junior citizens preparing for the use of the ballot, and for receiving the responsibility of senior citizenship. Make up your minds now that when the time comes you are going to pay your poll tax every year and vote in every election. If you'd start as early wanting to know how to use the ballot as you do wanting to learn how to drive, we'd never have to worry about keeping our freedom.

Your fathers and mothers are members of a generation that has been comparatively lax in its responsibility to government — and you are the ones who can straighten it out. The way to a man's citizenship is through his children — your interests are his interests. Even though you are not old enough to vote yet, you can prepare for the time when you will vote, and you can actually begin voting now — through your influence. Use your influence for good government. Take your parents to school meetings and programs, and to political rallies — get them interested in public affairs. They'll do more for you than you think! If they say they are too busy, form a citizenship partnership with your parents — be their reporter; keep them informed so that they can form intelligent opinions. Instead of bringing home the latest jive record, bring home the Congressional Record. Give Father the comics and you take the editorials.

Third Step — Team America — Jump in and Solve Today's Problems Together

I have a light-hearted statement that I sometimes use when speaking publicly about "youth being able to cipher correctly so they can ensure that my Social Security checks are correct and timely." Well the truth is that we must fix the seemingly insurmountable challenges we have today as an American Team - all generations working together to set it right. Imagine how powerful that approach will be!

The Chancellor of the University of Texas (UT) system, former Navy Admiral Bill McRaven, has announced that UT will pursue a "team of teams" approach. That's exactly what I am suggesting here for youth in the New Americanism. The binding together of existing generations to solve problems indeed requires a team of teams approach so that it can be durable and sustainable in its solutions. Just consider each generations as a team and you get the picture.

Team Youth should also focus on examining the issues of Team Elderly because it would have many benefits for both teams. Youth could understand much better what the elderly's requirements are so that they could start fashioning durable systems now that could work for them when they become elderly. For example, Social Security was a government idea in the mid-1930s. There will be other and better solutions for the future. It will take a team of teams to find out what these new solutions will look like and how they will function.

Team Youth are currently coming together in many communities creating clubs such as the Young Professionals of a given locale, or a city's Youth Leadership Club, along with similar organizations. They are doing so because of their perceived need to lead and take on the important issues of their communities together. I encourage these groups and help integrate them wherever possible so that they can start to learn what works best from each other – somewhat of a sharing of best practices. As we have seen the civic groups of our past nearly disappear, they are being replaced by new ones with different names and different charters. Team Baby Boomers needs to involve itself within these groups a lot more often. Award-winning actress, author and fitness icon Raquel Welch says, "60% of Americans are Boomers, and yet they are all but invisible in the popular media and American culture." That has got to change in the New Americanism.

Encourage a Reading Rebirth

Team Elderly can help Team Youth by encouraging them to read. Reading a short post or article online does not have the same learning and retention quality as reading this book. Watching a movie just isn't the same experience for one's brain as reading a book. Here's why: when you read a book, the words and their arrangement evoke reflection in the part of the brain that thinks and remembers. In other words, a person generates a "visual" in the brain while reading. That visual is retained far longer than by any other medium of reception. Watching a movie simply generates emotion more than anything else.

There is a proven difference between reading a printed document and reading something on-screen. For some biological reason, reading on-screen is not nearly as powerful as reading a printed document. I am somewhat traditional in this regard. If someone wants me to critically read something that they've written, I always print it out first and read the printed copy. There is no precise substitute for the powerful effect and value of reading printed matter.

Parents can help by selecting a book, reading it first, and then passing it along to their children. After the children have read it, it can become dinner conversation, thereby reinforcing the learning value and critical thinking brought about by the book. Each family member could have a different take or perspective on a particular part of the book. Discussing the differing viewpoints brings about the greatest level of learning and enlightenment. Turn off the TV and start having some very interesting dinner conversations about the New Americanism!

My Grandson's Thoughts

Christian Harvey read this chapter with great interest, After all, I am writing about his generation. This is what he shared:

> I agree! It's not our fault that we were raised to be dependent on technology. Also, we are using these resources to try and fix the problems that older people have created in America. So cut us a break!

Summary

Youth today are the future guarantors of American liberty and freedom. I look forward to the future, and seeing Team Youth achieve many triumphs over adversity — with Team Elderly's help. After all, youth weren't the ones to get our nation into nearly $20 trillion of debt. They bought into the dream of education but sometimes at the cost of massive student debt. In the race toward greatness, their starting line has been moved back somewhat because of the legacies they are inheriting from preceding generations.

It's disheartening to see millennials lose the American dream of home ownership. In many cases, they can't come up with the down payments required to secure mortgages for homes. Some state legislatures, such as Connecticut, are considering bills that reduce a millennial's personal income liability by 10% of their annual mortgage payments, up to $1200. This amounts to a *hand up*, not a *hand out*.

I inherited a strong America from my parents in the 1950s. Credit usage was nearly non-existent, and the "Red Menace" (Communism), along with the hydrogen bomb, commonly referred to as "the H-bomb", seemed to be the only things we had looming over us – oh, and maybe a few aliens too. I learned how to be a citizen starting in the 3rd and 4th grades and learned to respect the values that made post-World War II America so great. But the American dream demands that our children do better than we did and right now that's not looking so promising.

We must bind together with the younger generations and tell them how important their task is. We must help them materially to solve large, complex problems – any other approach would amount to abandonment. We can do this – it starts now.

Chapter 14

Choosing the Next President – Why Leadership Matters.

If your actions inspire others to dream more, learn more, do more and become more, you are a leader.
— John Quincy Adams

What kind of leader *should* the next president be? What kind of leader does the next president of the United States *need* to be? You might like the first question rather the second if you are *concerned* about America. If, however, you are *worried* about America, you're probably more inclined to favor the wording of the second question.

The New Americanism demands that we favor strong language concerning the leadership of our next president – he or she must be a very particular type of leader so that the United States may experience a transition to our next phase of greatness and exceptionalism. We need him or her to possess a natural set of predispositions as a leader and a history of cultivating them into repeated and consistent behaviors. We need for the president to be less of an ideologue and more of a uniter. And we need all this at the outset of the president's first term. No "on-the-job training" will suffice. No amount of surrounding oneself with smart people will work. The president really needs to be accomplished from the beginning, understand how to lead, in small settings, in large groups, and on the world scene.

The status quo will not suffice.

Ignoring the leadership issue and hoping it will go away will not suffice.

Taking on a president who does not understand the nature of 21st century leadership will not suffice.

We find ourselves well into the 21st century already, and we continue to seek either a "return to the good old days" or a "bold leap into the future". Both of these general strategies will not work. We live and must understand "the fierce urgency of now" as Dr. Martin Luther King stated. The next president must live *in the moment* almost every waking hour of every day – something that is much more difficult to do than talking about a glorified past or future.

Each time I hear an elected leader talk about how great the past was or conversely, how great the future will be, I tend to cringe because these remarks are nearly always a tacit avoidance of the fierce urgency of now.

The Nature of Leadership

As the leader of an organization charged with teaching leadership, ethics, and service to the youth of Texas, it is naturally my job to understand leadership in depth. I believe that there are a number of different ways to accomplish that in-depth learning. These ways are applied in combination for maximum effect.

The first thing that must be accomplished is to understand what leadership is all about, what it is intrinsically, and be able to define it in several different ways. It's difficult to define, not because we lack the right words, but rather because by defining leadership we actually confine it too much. We exclude elements by our definitions that might be included in reality. In Kantian philosophy, leadership might very well be what he called a "noumenon". Without being too abstract, a noumenon can be thought of as the *thing itself* – not the thing as we observe it or know it or understand it through the application of our senses.

That's why we favor studying and explaining leadership through its application in our behaviors every day. I intend to talk about leadership as a set of observable behaviors – because really that's the only thing that counts for most of us – the behaviors.

Do I blaspheme for suggesting to ignore chasing down a pristine and unchallengeable definition of leadership in our world? Perhaps, but I think not. If you want one of those, please skip ahead to Chapter 15, then return here.

Like many of you, I've been to many leadership conferences and events, read books about leadership, and listened to "experts" talk about leadership. All of these are somewhat helpful but beware of some of those experts – they employ some pretty slick techniques to build their followings, write glitzy books from a "self-help" perspective, and wow you at their conferences.

One of these experts has written so many self-help type books, published a wealth of multimedia "leadership ware", and lives on the lecture circuit. You might say that writing leadership books and talking about leadership to large numbers of people is his life's calling. I have been to two of his lectures. He employs a lot of *visual speech* such as likening his comments to *nuggets of gold* and feigns throwing those nuggets at you while you are sitting in the audience. His sessions pretty much make you feel good and comfortable with yourself, and you leave thinking that you've been enlightened and empowered.

Beware of what I call "pop culture leadership". You can always identify these types of leadership experts because they love finite lists to try and explain leadership. It sounds like this usually:

> "Here, my friends, are the three things you must do to become a great leader."
> "Blog post: The Top Five Things not to do as a Leader."
> "Article: The Ten Most Powerful Attributes of Great Leaders"

Go ahead and review those lists, but rest assured that leadership comes alive in you by what you decide to do, not by living vicariously through the leadership lists of others. And we are only interested in your own personal leadership behaviors because these will determine your effectiveness when in leadership positions.

If you absolutely insist on having a *leadership list*, I won't disappoint. Although I would call these things the important parts of leadership — the *right stuff* that constitutes very good leaders.

The first large part of what makes up a leader can be referred to as "disposition" or "inclination to act". Leaders understand that their backgrounds, personalities, upbringing, values, belief systems, culture and environment definitely affect the way that they are inclined to act in any given situation. It's really what distinguishes various leaders from one another.

The second big part of what makes up a leader is action and behavior. It's the visible part of our leadership, the tip of the iceberg. It's the part that is constantly observable and open to judgment, approval, or criticism.

The third component of great leadership is the leader's motivation to act. Although that motivation can be somewhat invisible, it is important because the leader's actions should achieve a beneficial impact for a lot of people. It must strengthen a societal good. Consider the "4-Way Test" that Rotarians recite at the close of every meeting:

> Is it the TRUTH?
> Is it FAIR to all concerned?
> Will it build GOODWILL and BETTER FRIENDSHIPS?
> Will it be BENEFICIAL to all concerned?

Before we continue to look at how leadership should best be understood and practiced in the 21st century, let's just summarize the three time-honored components of great leadership:

Leadership Dispositions – the Inclination to Act in a Certain Manner

Shakespeare said, "Some men were born great, some achieve greatness and others have greatness thrust upon them."

So leadership is all about behavior, huh? Yup. But there's something in any social system that comes just before the behavior, or action. There are a series of dispositions or inclinations that we all have inside of us that make it likely that we'll act in one way or another. These dispositions are acquired over the first part of our lives, generally from birth to our early twenties. They are engrained into us through our experiences. They make it so that our behaviors, or visible actions, can be somewhat predictable if we can identify the particular dispositions that come into play.

Donald Trump was raised in an entrepreneurial business environment where he acquired dispositions to act in a particular way. You have to be tough to succeed in that world so he learned to be tough and outsmart the competition. He learned the art of the deal and how to out-negotiate adversaries. Therefore, Mr. Trump is inclined to act in ways that someone with his experience set would naturally have.

Hillary Clinton was raised in the dog-eat-dog world of career politicians. Her dispositions appear to be coming out of those experiences. Pleasant, smiling, and accommodating on the outside but take-no-prisoners on the inside. Her verbal communications have the style of a lifelong politician. She is predisposed to act far differently than Mr. Trump because of her political background—taking into account the possible reactions of her pronouncements on her base, the opposition, and every other group of people.

Understanding a leader's motivation to act in a certain way helps us to predict that person's inclination to make a decision one way or another. Which leader is true to his or her beliefs? Which one panders to the audience that he or she happens to be speaking to at the moment? Which one understands the most about American values and principles?

Leadership Actions – They are the Only Things that Matter to Others

You know the old saying: "He's a legend in his own mind." We all can be great leaders and members of society in our own minds, but that doesn't count for much at all. Only action changes things. That change can make things better or worse, but only action can bring about change. President Obama has often been lauded as a great speaker – having the ability to emotionally connect to his audience, deliver a message in an emotionally powerful way that causes the audience to feel a certain way. President Reagan also had that same ability. The big difference between the two however, is that there was effective follow-through on the part of President Reagan, working extensively to promote his agenda through the House and the Senate. He forged alliances with key legislators to get things done.

President Obama on the other hand, delivered great speeches but did not follow up with the necessary work and deliberations required to forge consensus throughout both house of Congress. I suppose if I were to ask him about that, he may say, "You're wrong, I did follow up" but the fact is that as president, one has to persevere in follow-up until a beneficial conclusion is reached. It's simply not enough to write executive decisions and mandates that do not have the power of enacted laws and which disappear upon a change of administration. To do so is tantamount to imposing one man's view of how we should live on every American. Polarization therefore occurs, with each political party blaming the other for these failures.

One could also think of this in terms of span of impact. A speech could reach a national audience but these words tend to waft off into the atmosphere and become lost after some time elapses. When I speak to audiences, I sometimes remind them that they will most likely forget a lot of what I've said a few days after my remarks, and that they must enact leadership into their behaviors so as to make it theirs and make those behaviors durable. A speech only serves as a catalyst for thought. It must be followed up with action – every bit as much as a phone call might be followed by an email, which in turn could engender a committee to bring about action.

Leadership Motivations - Our Behaviors must be Borne from a Desire to Help Others and make Things Better for Everyone

Our need to do the right thing, ethics and service, is undeniable and a huge part of how well the impact of our leadership actions is distributed. Ethics is all about *doing the right thing*. I have found that some people shy away from the study of ethics, fearing that it's a complex topic that only the brightest of philosophers can hope to understand. Nothing could be farther from the truth. Ethics is being true to our nature as human beings. Most of us want to do the right thing and want to serve others.

I think that most every U.S. president arrives in office wanting to do the right thing and definitely understands that there are universally right things – not culturally or contextually right. For example, to treat others the way you wish to be treated can be construed as a universalism.

The Nature of Leadership in Our Times

We are living in complexity. I'm not simply talking about complicated – that's a different word with a totally different meaning. Complexity, in the systems context, is when there are many more independent variables than dependent ones. Just to keep this discussion clear and simple, it means that it's much harder to control and predict the course of our social system and all its artifacts than ever before.

The Imperialist Presidency – Revisited

Even though he is convinced that he is doing the right thing, President Obama is imposing his own worldview and perspectives on all of us each time that he signs an executive order that has a fairly large impact. That is not ethical because it runs contrary to how our system was designed by the Constitution's authors. It's exactly contrary to the spirit and the law of the land which set up bicameral houses (two separate legislative bodies), and branches of government to have a system of checks and balances.

To use executive orders, in the place of what should be properly passed laws, is the key issue.

The other side of the coin is that the president cites the inability of the current *do nothing* Congress to pass effective legislation and the predisposition of that Congress to oppose anything that he comes up with. Even if those two suppositions were largely true, it would not provide him with some type of rationale based on frustration to revert to the unethical use of executive orders. Again, when I say "unethical" I mean employing executive orders that have a significant societal impact, such as immigration policy. Those are clearly in the realm of legislation.

Congress has the power to overturn an executive order by passing legislation in conflict with it. Congress can also refuse to provide funding necessary to carry out certain policy measures contained with the order, or to legitimize policy mechanisms.

Our Ideal Leader

This is one of those discussions that rises above party politics so if you are expecting me to espouse a particular ideology when I talk about leadership, most likely you will be disappointed. Real leadership transcends all ideology.

As stated previously, we need a leader with a reflective mind – someone that demonstrates an even keel, especially in the face of crisis. We need a leader who can remain calm under duress. Someone who by remaining calm and intact inspires others who might be on the verge of falling apart just when we need them to keep it together. Otherwise said, we need a leader with a mature temperament.

We are looking for a president with courage. Having courage to act and take a stand is very admirable and it inspires confidence. Even when we don't agree on the stance taken, we generally tend to respect the fact that the president has a clear position on a given crisis or issue. Very few people will follow someone who doesn't know where he is going. We want a president with courage to establish a vision and the perseverance to go after it. We don't need someone who follows too closely his poll or popularity numbers.

We want a president who has a great sense of humor. Humor is that special quality of leadership that transcends a lot of problems and puts people at ease. Humor can break through an apparent policy road block in a heartbeat. Humor is infectious and causes us to feel good about the person who employs it. For example, President Reagan often used humor to his advantage many times during his presidency – and it served him well. Humor has to come from the heart – it can't be forced or artificial and we sure can recognize forced humor when we see it. The president does not need to be joker-in-chief, but he or she does need to lighten up the room, rather than suck all the air out of it, so that people can feel comfortable enough to contribute.

We don't necessarily need an intellectual for our next president – but we do need someone with common sense. Our presidents have come from all walks of life and the next one doesn't need to be a lawyer and doesn't need to be an Ivy League alum. It's okay if he or she is, just not necessary or any more desirable than other presidential characteristics. Stateswoman Sarah Palin says that it's helpful if presidents have experience at the lower levels of government. Such experience can help them to connect with others, work together, be more civil, and employ common sense. Again, there is no hard fast rule on this but it certainly would help.

We want our next president to demonstrate humility. No one expects a president to be a paragon of perfection, so why try to create and give the impression that you can do no wrong? If you are wrong just admit it and move on. We only care that you learn from your mistake. We admire humble people. It's a universal leadership trait historically. Being a servant leader is a prescription for success at the highest office in the land.

There is one no-defects area of leadership, though: ethics. Once ethics are compromised, it's almost impossible build back up the level of trust necessary to be an effective leader. We need a moral leader with an unwavering code of ethics. Someone that would do the same thing when no one is looking. Let's hope that we elect someone who understands that the truth reigns supreme when you've got the responsibility of the world's finest nation in your charge. This includes not committing *sins of omission* – leaving essential truths unsaid because they would not put the president in a good light.

Lastly, we need a uniter, not a divider. We don't need someone who takes every opportunity to create needless and endless classes of people within our society and try to then cater to each one differently. We just need for everyone to be recognized as equal and for the president to be the president of everyone. No more visits to the White House by people who have an axe to grind on a particular social issue. The president just can't involve himself in every news event out there – he must show restraint and remain above those issues – not immediately jump in the fray. That type of presidential behavior only serves to polarize us even more than we are now.

Summary

Great 21st century style leadership is essential to the New Americanism. We need leaders who understand the level of complexity that we live in and can be agile enough to respond quickly. We don't need curmudgeons who are stuck in the last century and who think that what worked in the past will work now. The art of leadership is inserting oneself without inserting oneself. It's developing the leadership potential of others, fostering the creating of new leaders who will then, in turn, solve big problems while creating more leaders themselves.

Chapter 15

Taking the New Americanism Home

> I don't know much about Americanism, but it's a damn good word with which to carry an election.
> — Warren G. Harding

All the nice words and good intentions that you may have developed after reading about the New Americanism are worth nothing without action. Action truly is the most important part of leadership because without it, nothing happens and nothing changes. It's appropriate, therefore, to position the concept of *Taking It Home* as the last chapter of the New Americanism.

Taking it home was an often-used phrase of former Attorney General of Texas John Ben Shepperd to indicate applying one's beliefs and leadership learning in community; to transform your words and intentions into action for the betterment of everyone. He especially coached young Texans to develop their leadership and "taking it home" skills early, saying:

> Don't wait until you're 21 to be a citizen. A football player doesn't wait until he has the ball to start warming up on the sidelines. He does the warming up before he gets into the game. When you reach 21 you've got to be ready to run with the ball. Get off the sidelines and warm up for citizenship. Maybe you've been saying, "When I get to be 21 I'm going to be a good citizen. I'm going to do things." If that's your symptom, you have a common teen-age disease, "21-itis." You're putting everything off until a future date. But turning 21 won't cure you. When that time comes you will say, "I won't vote this time. The important elections don't come up till next year. I won't write my Congressman—he wouldn't listen to a mere taxpayer anyway." If you don't get a shot in the arm now, you'll have 21-itis the rest of your life. (Brescia, 2015)

The concept of applying one's leadership in community is directly linked to our definition of leadership itself:

> "Leadership is the *demonstrated ability* to *set direction, mobilize commitment,* and *build capabilities* toward a *shared goal.*"

Demonstrated Ability

Many people believe that they are leaders in their own minds; if only others would just follow. Well, real leadership calls for demonstrated ability – visible to all. Action nearly always has the component of intent – You intend to do something and then you do it. On occasion we float our intents to others so as to elicit a reaction. For example, I sometimes write an email to particular stakeholders of my leadership institute that starts out, "I intend to…" and then describe the particular approach or initiative that we wish to undertake. That's the first step. If everyone's input or concerns have been understood and accommodated, then I take the action – the final step. No one really cares too much about what you say – but they sure care about what you do because actions can have positive, negative, individual and collective consequences whereas intent has none of those.

Set Direction

Setting direction is simply establishing a vision that you follow and others can choose to follow as well. The lack of vision can be very troubling and even crippling in the New Americanism because almost no one lines up behind a person who lacks vision. What's your vision for personal and professional success? What's your vision for your community? How about your vision for your family? The stronger and more compelling that your vision is, the more it will take hold and become a beacon for others.

In public service, the statesmen and politicians who establish a great vision for their constituents or for the office that they seek to hold, are generally the ones that prevail. The ones that simply run campaigns that bash everyone else are those that are incomplete and risk failure. People want to know what candidates will do on their behalf, not how a candidate feels about another candidate. Of course, candidates must be comparative on occasion, pointing out their strengths as compared to the other candidates but they should spend twice that amount of energy and time in driving home their vision for the future.

Mobilize Commitment

A New Americanism leader must use positive influence to ensure completion of the goal. This is done by effectively communicating the message about the vision, as far and wide as possible. Note also that commitment is a very strong word, and a lot stronger word than just simple awareness.

Build Capabilities

This is usually done directly after gaining commitment but can also be started at the same time. This is the step that often falls apart because it's sometimes difficult to effectively accomplish. Leaders must provide the right context for followers to accomplish the mission and they must obtain adequate resources for them to employ. Anything short of that reeks of abandonment, or failed empowerment. One can empower others, but if the resources are lacking then it amounts to simple abandonment.

Shared Goal

It's essential that the New Americanism leader's goal is a shared one with followers – anything short of that would be unethical. For example, a U.S. Representative typically takes great pains to ensure that there is alignment between the bills that he works on in Washington, D.C. and the general interests of the district that he represents.

There are many places to begin taking it home in community. You can start small and then build up a number of different ways to help your community to be a better one for everybody. For example, you could offer your services to help sort donations and then stock them on the shelves of the local thrift shops. You could volunteer at the local animal rescue facility. How about coaching a sports team for the YMCA? It's really up to you and a simple Internet search should provide you with all of the information that you need in your locality to begin taking it home.

Taking it home is truly a cornerstone of the New Americanism because Americans help each other. We don't need the government to help us – we just need to help each other and especially those who have the most need. Taking it home should be the norm and not the exception. Imagine if almost every person felt a mandate to help others in community to the best of his ability – far fewer government programs and services would be needed and therefore the overall cost of government could be significantly reduced. The quality of such assistance would also be significantly improved as well. Americans are helpers and givers. We all need to be true to ourselves and those qualities to make the New American flourish and grow.

It is our habit at most Texas Leadership Forums to match well-established leaders, politicians, statesmen, and appointed officials with younger, aspiring leaders. Throughout the first part of the conference, they attend sessions together and share a wealth of ideas on the pressing issues of our times in the Lone Star State. It's amazing to see the verbal exchange among younger and older leaders – and it's also quite enriching. Generally on the last day of the conference, we invite participants to describe their learnings and tell us how they intend to *take it home*. What project will they undertake in their communities and how will they accomplish them? We then track that progress and at the following annual conference examine the results. In this way, conference attendance is much more powerful than just being there and then letting it all go subsequently.

The New Americanism calls for action, not just understanding. Only action can result in change and only change can result in progress. I truly hope that every reader of this book takes it home and starts a revolution in Americanism in their communities. Start a movement to do something that you know needs to be done. Volunteer your time in a civic organization. Visit your school superintendent and find out how you can help to supplement civics education. Mentor someone who really needs it. Identify an elderly person or couple who needs someone to help out with the things they can no longer do. Be the change you want to see in everyone else and in our system

Summary — The Celebration of the New Americanism

Americanism is as old as America itself. Throughout the years since our inception Americanism has drawn the attention of friends and enemies alike. Consider this German propaganda, written during 1944, which demonstrated Nazi dislike for our culture and what we stand for:

> The only remaining alternative is Americanism. As strange as it may sound, it is the only serious competition to National Socialism's racial worldview in the struggle

for the youth, in the struggle for the future of humanity. In the end, however, it is only a forerunner of Bolshevism.

Americanism is certainly not a spiritual movement, nor is it a worldview that it is possible to oppose at the intellectual level. Its political beneficiaries have tried in recent years to give it, if not a face, at least a program or a goal: "the American Century." It is a collection of empty promises of the type democratic orators have always made — but this time on a world scale. There is nothing in them to excite a reasonable man. But that is exactly the point of Americanism! The key is not what it promises, but what it cannot promise. The key is not what it demands of men, but what gives them (Korps, 1944).

The New Americanism calls for a 100% total commitment – you are either in or out, with no in-between. No saying that you will participate some of the time or if it's convenient to do so. We need Americans who are true believers in Americanism. If we had a whole nation of those, we would be untouchable for thousands of years to come.

You can't betray the New Americanism and expect to be subsequently considered an American. If you betray your country and its values, you cannot be extended any further rights or privileges of

U.S. citizenship. For example, in March 2016, a young American by the name of Mohamad Jamal Khweis from Alexandria, Virginia turned himself into Kurdish forces, saying that he had made "a bad decision" to join the American Islamic State fighters. A bad decision indeed, to renounce one's country and then expect it to welcome you back with open arms. Once an American crosses lines like that, such behavior is traitorous and that person should lose U.S. citizenship forever.

We need to celebrate and highlight our achievements a whole lot more in the New Americanism – the good things that we are doing, not the bad ones. Let's celebrate our principles and values unabashedly and place them on the top shelf. Sure – we are going to have failures and misses as we strive to be the best we can be. Those misses are not representative of who we are as a people, and therefore, they should be placed on lower shelves. Our misses, flaws, and mistakes don't need to be thrown in our faces every time they occur or held up to the rest of the world to gaze upon. That's not hiding our mistakes – it's simply choosing to make our successes and our exceptionalism a lot more visible to all.

Let's condemn mediocrity in all its forms. The media can help by offering many more positive, human-achievement oriented stories rather than the constant stream of bad news. We are often treated to pointless television reports about well-known personalities in the entertainment industry. Those stories have little value in our lives. Ask your local channels to accentuate the optimistic, positive side of the news. Ask the station manager to be a proponent of reversing the "if it bleeds, it leads" nature of the news. This will be a slow process to be sure but it has to start somewhere. The New Americanism seeks out bravery, truth, and examples of service to others.

For example, if you are looking for stories about real bravery, then feature some of our nation's military members and veterans. You may not only find true bravery but you could find a way to help those brave people reintegrate effectively back into the communities that they came from. If you were to do some of those things, then you would be brave, too – and a great American. How about a story on the Girl Scout Troop in Midland, Texas that started a free book library for the community?

All stories don't have to be heroic. For example, there is our granddaughter Reagan's story – at age 11, she was in an elevator with us and a significantly handicapped older gentleman. He could not manage to select the right floor button. Reagan immediately acted to help him. When she did, her tablet computer fell from her hands and hit the floor. It was cracked and inoperable. We were so pleased at her instant willingness to help others that we helped her – and replaced her tablet with a new one.

When the John Ben Shepperd Public Leadership Institute expressed the desire to get an oil portrait done to celebrate our namesake's commemorative 100th birthday last year, Lubbock, Texas, artist Bo Tan (www.botanstudio.com) volunteered to donate his time and talent to get the job done. Bo is a great American of Chinese descent who celebrates living here and who, with his wonderful wife, has raised a super son, George. George has served his country in both Afghanistan and Iraq. In spite of the many demands on his time, George helps his father with the studio and is now very involved in civic projects within our community. The Tan family is truly an exemplar of celebrating the New Americanism.

Another great story comes to us from the heartland of the United States—Poplar Bluff, Missouri. My wife and I drove from our home in Texas to Poplar Bluff to attend the funeral of her Uncle—Donnie Hornbeck. Donnie's daughter and only child, Ms. Debbie Trout, is a wonderful cousin and true friend. Her dad led an admirable life—service in the Armed Forces and then service to the school district for many years. He was a perfect exemplar of a great American. From the moment we entered the town of Poplar Bluff, we were awestruck by the kindness of those we met there—they were truly welcoming, warm, and genuinely friendly. They understood and practiced the American value of benevolence. We had the great opportunity to have dinner with several of the ladies that serve in the

Poplar Bluff courthouse. What fine examples they all were of service and benevolence to others — truly unsung heroes of the New Americanism.

The time soon came for the service and funeral for Uncle Donnie. At Cousin Debbie's request, Marianne sat next to her, facing the flag-draped casket, under the funeral tent on the grounds of the Poplar Bluff City Cemetery. It was raining that day. Others stood around the tent with umbrellas — I stood nearby so that I could capture some video with my phone. The local Army Reserve provided three soldiers and a firing party because Donnie was a veteran and the family highly respected his service to country. The soldiers did an excellent job of carrying out their ceremonial duties. Everything proceeded as expected. The firing party fired their shots skyward and then it happened. At the very moment that the last shot was fired, the skies instantly cleared up and the sun burst through the clouds — but mostly right on Uncle Donnie's flag-draped casket. The sun's rays appeared to be focused on that casket — several in attendance were visibly stunned. Marianne and Debbie exchanged glances and squeezed each other's hands in recognition that something extraordinary had just occurred. To me, it was almost as if the Lord had sent Donnie that message that we all want to hear when we pass, "Well done, my good and faithful servant."

The skies went back to gray and light rain ensued. That moment of sunshine lent clarity to the spirit of Americanism that permeated throughout the entire Hornbeck family. From the American Revolutionary War service of Sergeant Benjamin Hornbeck, to the Civil War, and in present times, the great American Hornbeck family served in defense of our nation. Marianne's dad Ira served twice in Vietnam where he was exposed to deadly Agent Orange which caused the cancer that took him away from his family. Ira's brother Everett was a prisoner of war in World War II. Brother Donnie served in the Army during the Korean Conflict and brothers Jesse and Carl in World War II. Brother Ralph served in the Army as well. The family's heritage and legacy is one of defending our freedom and liberty by serving in uniform — for the good of all Americans.

Stateswoman Wendy Davis from Texas has the right idea about *taking it home*. Wendy has started a social movement centered on women's rights, equality of the sexes, equal pay for equal work, LGBTQ inclusion, and other social issues. It's called, "Deeds Not Words" (www.deedsnotwords.com) and it's growing rapidly. Her basic idea is that if we join forces, find tools, and take action, things will actually improve - initiatives will happen and progress will be made. Deeds Not Words provides a great platform for those wishing to go beyond the good thoughts of doing great things together. Wendy Davis's initiative is an excellent example of people binding together to *take it home*. The New Americanism is very inclusive – every American has the potential to be a *great* American – movements like Wendy's show you how to transform words into action.

Here is another bit of advice for anyone wishing to join in and celebrate the New Americanism: always make it a point to widen the breadth of the news and other media content that reaches your eyes and ears. If you only listen to, watch, and read news sources that you tend to agree with, you are setting yourself up with an ideology problem. Make at least one of your news sources an "antagonistic" one. For example, when I was an executive at Michelin North America in Greenville, South Carolina, we lived on Lake Keowee in Seneca – a 50-minute drive. During my morning commute, I listened to National Public Radio (NPR). For my evening commute, I tuned my car radio to generally conservative talk shows. By so doing, it became routine for me to reflect on several different perspectives on the news. A final point about what you "ingest" with respect to media – nothing beats the printed word. If you really want to be an exceptional New American, cultivate your reading habits because it is the best way to cause deeper thought and reflection on the issues.

The New Americanism works. The New Americanism is based on tried and true values and principles. The road ahead will be a thrilling ride – twists and turns, slips and falls, triumphs and tragedies – but it's our American ride and we will prevail.

What's next?

You've read the book and are excited about the prospect of the New Americanism. You wish that our politicians, statesmen, and appointed officials practiced a lot of what is contained in this book. You want others to read these pages and then act on these precepts.

Like most change initiatives and as the saying goes, we must first be the change that we wish to see in others. So our daily behaviors must extoll the virtues of the New Americanism and be readily visible for others to see. Join, or create, civic clubs that can become New Americanism chapters. Make it a family project. Write your elected officials and tell them that you believe in the New Americanism. Then we have to create more believers through conversation and sharing so that they too can discover all the wonderful things that we can achieve as Americans working together.

Don't back away from the effort or wither under any criticism that may come your way because of your beliefs. Stand tall and proud that you are a great American. Our greatest days have yet to come

– the present is our *now* in which we will set the cornerstones of the greatest nation on Earth. May God continue to bless these United States and may we bless each other with the power of knowledge, respect, understanding, and greatness.

Bob Brescia

REFERENCES

Abbott, J. (2010). *Ethics: An Early American Handbook*: ReadaClassic.com.
Associated_Press. (2016). DC Myor Bans City Workers from Travel to North Carolina. Retrieved from http://abcnews.go.com/US/wireStory/dc-mayor-bans-city-workers-travel-north-carolina-38084275
Brescia, R. (2015). The Americanism of John Ben Shepperd (1st ed.). Conshohocken, PA: Infinity Publishing.Halfacre, S. (2016). *Gingrich Speks on Civility in Politics*. Retrieved from http://easttennessean.com/2016/04/04/newt-gingrichs-take-on-civility-in-politics/.
Concha, J. (2016, February 26, 2016). Harris-Perry Throws Away TV Career, Petulantly Plays Race Card From Bottom of the Deck. *Medialite*.
Editors, T. (2011). The New Americanism. *America - The National Catholic Review*.Fingerhut, H. (2015). Millennials' Views of News Media, Religious Organizations Grow More Negative. *Fact Tank: News in the Numbers*.

Frost, D. (1968). *The Presidential Debate, 1968*. New York: Stein and Day.

Gelernter, D. (2007). *Americanism: The Fourth Great Western Religion*: Doubleday.

Johnson, P. (2007). Heroes: What Great Statesmen Have to Teach Us. *Imprimis*, 36(12). Retrieved from https://imprimis.hillsdale.edu/heroes-what-great-statesmen-have-to-teach-us/

Landers, L. (Writer). (1947). The Son of Rusty.

Mckay, B. K. (2012). The Four Qualities of a True Statesman. Retrieved from http://www.naturalawakeningsmag.com/Natural-Awakenings/October-2012/The-Four-Qualities-of-a-True-Statesman/

Miller, K. (2016). LePage refuses to swear in senator-elect over spat with Democrats. *The Portland Press Herald*. Retrieved from http://www.pressherald.com/2016/04/01/lepage-refuses-to-swear-in-senator-elect-over-spat-with-democrats/

New Research Confirms the Power of Debate to Change Lives. (2016). Retrieved from http://chicagodebateleague.org/new-research-confirms-the-power-of-debate-to-change-lives/

Palin, S. (2015) *Civility in Leadership/Interviewer: D. R. Brescia*.

Press, A. (2016). Long-term Elderly Care Sees Growing Demand. http://oaoa.tx.newsmemory.com/publink.php?shareid=25ad883aa Retrieved from http://oaoa.tx.newsmemory.com/publink.php?shareid=25ad883aa

Schultz, H. (2016). Howard Schultz Calls for Civility and Values-Based Leadership [Press release]. Retrieved from https://news.starbucks.com/news/Howard-Schultz-on-role-and-responsibility-of-citizens

Syrmopoulos, J. (2015). The Power of Knowledge: Harvard Debate Team Loses to Prison Debate Team. Retrieved from http://thefreethoughtproject.com/prison-debate-team-beats-harvard/

Warren, R. (2002). *A Purpose Driven Life*. Grand Rapids, Michigan: Zondervan.

Washington, G. (Year Unknown). George Washington's Rules of Civility and Decent Behavior in Company and Conversation. Stilwell, KS: DigiReads.com. (Reprinted from: Applewood Books).

Endorsements

"Americanism is something I grew up with in my little hometown in Arkansas. We saluted the flag. We respected those in authority, be it a soldier, a teacher, a police officer, or our parents. We prayed at public events. We gave generously to causes that cured diseases, fed the hungry, put clothes on kids, educated a child, or saved souls. When the National Anthem was played, we stopped in our tracks, took off our hats, and stood at attention with our right hand over our hearts. It wasn't unique to Hope, Arkansas. But it was unique to America. Robert Brescia has captured more than a nostalgic look back, but a powerful look ahead at what the changes in our culture mean for America and Americanism. It's a compelling reminder of the greatness of America and why it matters that we keep it that way."

- Mike Huckabee
Former Governor of Arkansas and 2-time U.S. Presidential Candidate

"Powerful, succinct, to the point. Every American who wants an America we can respect and love should read and heed this book."

- Ben Stein
American writer, lawyer, actor, and political commentator

"Robert Brescia provides not only a wonderful history of the unique features of America's greatness, but also a roadmap for how we can revive a sense of Americanism. Dr. Brescia truly understands what currently ails our country - from a waning sense of patriotism to neglecting to teach the Constitution in our country's schools - and his proposals are exactly what our nation needs. This book is a must-read for anyone who believes that, with a little bit of hard work, America's best days are still ahead of us."

- Janine Turner
Actress, Founder and Co-Chair, Constituting America

"My appreciation for Americanism grows with each turned page of Destination Greatness. Dr. Brescia's inspiring words elevate us beyond our own mindsets. He reminds us that so much more important than whether we are liberal or conservative, is that we are Americans."

- Alan Colmes
American radio and television host, liberal political commentator

Bob Brescia's DESTINATION GREATNESS is a wonderful description of how America can be the nation she was designed as — powerful yet humble, demanding yet benevolent, accommodating but accountable. I have known Bob for several years and he's one of the true "Americanism" guys in our country today — believes and practices inclusion, civic responsibilities, community service, and helping those most in need. His book is essential reading for anyone seeking to be the great American that's inside all of us.

- Nirav Tolia
Founder and CEO, *Nextdoor* **- the Private Social Network for Your Neighborhood**

CPSIA information can be obtained
at www.ICGtesting.com
Printed in the USA
LVOW13*2105091116
512328LV00007B/8/P

9 781495 812378